WITHDRAWN

Yale Studies in English, 185

THE POLITICS OF
MILTON'S PROSE STYLE

Keith W. Stavely

New Haven and London   Yale University Press

1975

PR
3592
P64
S8

Published with assistance from the
foundation established in memory of
Oliver Baty Cunningham of the Class
of 1917, Yale College.

Library of Congress catalog card number: 74-20086
International standard book number: 0-300-01804-5

Designed by John O. C. McCrillis
and set in Bold Face One type.
Printed in the United States of America by
The Murray Printing Co., Forge Village, Mass.

Published in Great Britain, Europe, and Africa by
Yale University Press, Ltd., London.
Distributed in Latin America by Kaiman & Polon,
Inc., New York City; in Australasia and Southeast
Asia by John Wiley & Sons Australasia Pty. Ltd.,
Sydney; in India by UBS Publishers' Distributors Pvt.,
Ltd., Delhi; in Japan by John Weatherhill, Inc., Tokyo.

To My Mother
and
To the Memory of My Father (1907–1973)

CONTENTS

vii

ACKNOWLEDGMENTS

All quotations of Milton's prose in the first four chapters are taken from Complete Prose Works of John Milton, ed. Don M. Wolfe and others, 8 vols. (New Haven: Yale University Press, 1953–   ). Volume and page numbers are noted in the text at the end of each quoted passage. References to this edition in the notes are abbreviated to "PW " Volume 7 of the Yale edition, containing the tracts of 1659–60, was published after the present study was already in proof. For the analyses of these tracts in the fifth chapter, I have therefore used volume 6 of The Works of John Milton, ed. Frank Allen Patterson and others, 18 vols. (New York: Columbia University Press, 1931–38). In both text and footnotes this edition is abbreviated to "CM." I have followed Thomason's datings of individual tracts.

This work is the product of my education, both formal and informal, at Yale University and of my subsequent experiences as a teacher and citizen. I first learned to think and write about expository prose with the help of Martin Price and the late Rosalie Colie. Louis L. Martz supervised the development of my inchoate ideas on Milton's prose into a doctoral dissertation and later helped prepare the manuscript for submission to the Yale University Press. His assistance, immense and invaluable at every stage, can be but feebly recorded in a formal acknowledgment. Richard S. Sylvester and George deF. Lord read the manuscript for Yale Studies in English and provided me with comments which were unfailingly apt and useful. Bonnie Carroll typed the manuscript so beautifully that Nancy Paxton of Yale Press could concentrate exclusively on "the intricat and involv'd" excesses of my own expository prose.

I wish also to thank Maynard Mack, Jr., William G. Riggs, David Rubin, Jean M. Humez, Michael McKeon, and Sharon Cameron. Some of these friends gave my manuscript the direct and considerable benefit of their careful readings; all of them have influenced its substance indirectly—but nonetheless distinctly—by sharing with me the experience of studying literature, and beginning to teach it, in times which often demanded more immediate political action. Students in three undergraduate seminars likewise made significant though indirect contributions. My wife Patricia kept a straight face throughout.

In slightly altered form, section 2 of chapter 5 has already been published in Milton Studies 5 (1973). I am grateful for permission to reprint.

ix

INTRODUCTION

Some critics have regretted Milton's political prose; most have ignored it.[1] I am pleased to record Northrop Frye's handsome appreciation of it: "The complex historical issues and formidable titles of such works as Tetrachordon, Eikonoklastes, or Animadversions upon the Remonstrant's Defence often prevent us from discovering that they are brilliant polemical writings, crackling with wit and epigram and the free play of an exuberant and, granted the polemical context, good-humored mind."[2] That these left-handed productions might deserve such high aesthetic praise will not entirely surprise anyone who recalls Milton's primary reason for turning from poems to pamphlets in 1641: he says in the autobiographical sections of the antiprelatical tracts that the established order has made it difficult, if not impossible, for him to write the kind of deeply principled and heroic poetry he wishes to write. A reformed social order, Milton maintains, will be an imaginative social order, which is to say it will encourage true poets such as he hopes to become. Milton therefore finds himself obliged more perhaps than most other men to participate directly in the movement for social change, and for him this can only mean writing political pamphlets.[3] All this is not stated in so many words, but some such summary of Milton's political motives seems clearly to be implied by those extended revelations of literary aspiration which are placed otherwise so incongruously in the "troubl'd sea" of antiprelatical polemic. It would be startling, I think, if the political prose of a man who sees such close connections between poetry and politics were a "cool medium," notwithstanding the sharp distinction between poetry and prose Milton himself draws in The Reason of Church Government. I believe and will attempt to demonstrate in the following pages that Milton's prose is a medium of imaginative expression and that his tracts will therefore reward careful and sustained scrutiny by the literary critic. I conceive of this undertaking as paralleling in its method and purpose the detailed study John Holloway has made of the writings of The Victorian Sage.[4]

In his classic essay on "Politics and the English Language," George Orwell discerns an important relationship between political words and political deeds:

> The English language . . . becomes ugly and inaccurate because our thoughts are foolish, but the slovenliness of our language makes it easier for us to have foolish thoughts. The point is that the process is reversible. Modern English, especially written English, is full of bad habits which spread by imitation

1

and which can be avoided if one is willing to take the necessary
trouble. If one gets rid of these habits one can think more clearly, and to think clearly is a necessary first step towards political regeneration: so that the fight against bad English is not
frivolous and is not the exclusive concern of professional writers.[5]

This is more than excellent and cogent advice for all who take politics
seriously in the twentieth century. It is also the best justification I
have found for investigating the politics of prose style. The bulk of
Orwell's essay is devoted to critically examining selected examples
of modern political prose, in order to expose the political meaning of
such recurrent vices of modern English style as prolixity and euphe-
mism. Whatever the explicit content of his discourse, the "tired
hack," as Orwell calls him, is proposing to his reader or listener a
lifeless, dehumanized social order. Such are the politics of bureau-
cratic prose style.

This book is not about the political writing of a tired hack, to say
the least; but the strenuous vigor of Milton's prose style creates its
own set of political problems. I will be arguing that an exalted
"poetic" texture limits the political effectiveness of Milton's prose
instead of extending and enriching it. The literary "coherence" of
the individual pamphlet interferes with its "correspondence" to political reality, its sense of participation in the currents of actual political and social life.[6] Indeed, the coherence of individual sentences,
visionary conceits, or entire tracts works its absolute will on correspondence, absorbing social realities into imaginative patterns without
confronting and assessing those realities on their own terms. The
reader does not experience an imagined society which might develop
from the existing one; he is instead forced to disregard all that has
been and might plausibly be, and he finds in place of these absent
realities an exhilarating but fictional political vision.

Areopagitica and The Readie and Easie Way are the least effective
of Milton's prose works as political devices. Each is militantly ill-
timed in terms of the political situation, the former naively, the latter
ironically. And in each coherence fully dominates correspondence.
But these are Milton's two best prose works when judged by literary
standards. In making them so coherent, Milton systematically per-
forms the idealistic artist's task of legislating the world by imaginative fiat. Milton's political writings prepared him in this aesthetic
sense for his epic poetic legislations. But the qualities which would
achieve epic fulfillment in Paradise Lost were the same qualities
that limited the political utility of Milton's prose. Milton the prose
artist showed the way to Milton the blind bard, but Milton the citizen
and revolutionary activist could not work effectively for the only
revolution he believed in, a revolution that would liberate the poet.

SYNTAX AND PERSUASION

Milton and Renaissance Prose Styles

In the studies of seventeenth-century prose style that have appeared since Morris W. Croll's pioneering work on the subject, Milton has usually either been ignored or classified as a Ciceronian.[1] Milton indeed expressed his distaste for both the "loose" and "curt" varieties of the prevailing anti-Ciceronian fashion:

> He that cannot understand the sober, plain, and unaffected stile of the Scriptures, will be ten times more puzzl'd with the knotty Africanisms, the pamper'd metafors; the intricat, and involv'd sentences of the Fathers; besides the fantastick, and declamatory flashes; the crosse-jingling periods which cannot but disturb, and come thwart a setl'd devotion worse then the din of bells, and rattles. . . .
>
> I must confesse I took it as my part the lesse to endure that my respected friends through their own unnecessary patience should thus lye at the mercy of a coy flurting stile; to be girded with frumps and curtall gibes, by one who makes sentences by the Statute, as if all above three inches long were confiscat. [I:568, 872–73][2]

In another passage, in which he makes these same associations between anti-Ciceronian prose style and a perverse deviation from right reason and virtue, Milton contrasts such literary preferences and practices with his own warm approval of Cicero:

> How few among them that know to write, or speak in a pure stile, much lesse to distinguish the idea's, and various kinds of stile: in Latine barbarous, and oft not without solecisms, declaiming in rugged and miscellaneous geare blown together by the foure winds, and in their choice preferring the gay ranknesse of Apuleius, Arnobius, or any moderne fustianist, before the native Latinisms of Cicero. [I:934]

But we should be careful how we attach to a strongly individual literary temper such as Milton's a label that usually brings to mind the pedantic imitators of Cicero satirized by Erasmus. According to Croll, all the characteristic prose of the seventeenth century was anti-Ciceronian, "except the writings of one or two great individualists who escape the influence of their time" (p. 201). If this refers to Milton, it

should include a recognition of the obvious fact that Milton the poet
achieved individuality by his distinctive use of tradition. Similarly,
the individual voice of Milton the prose stylist is generated by an
interplay of Ciceronian and loose constructions.
George Williamson says that "Milton went to extremes in the Latin
mould, setting his Latin constructions against the idiom of the loose
period in English." In a footnote, after quoting C. E. Vaughan, he
places Milton's characteristic sentence forms between Hooker's elaborate suspensions and Browne's seemingly casual looseness:

'In Hooker the periodic structure—the "architectural pile," in
which the subordinate clauses are grouped symmetrically and
with strict logical sequence around the principal sentence—is
taken over bodily, or only with such modifications as the nature
of an uninflected language, like the English, imperatively requires. The result is magnificent, but it is undeniably an exotic.
In Milton the long sentence remains; on occasion it becomes even
longer. But the subordination of clause to clause is largely broken
through. Its place is taken by a far looser structure, of which the
guiding principle is co-ordination. The style of Milton, if techni-
cal terms may be forgiven, is in the main not syntactic but para-
tactic; not a synthesis of clauses, but an agglomeration.' If this
contrast appears in Milton, it is much more apparent and pervasive in Browne.[3]

More recently, K. G. Hamilton has described a typical Miltonic sentence as being "complex, mainly periodic, though with some balanced
or loose components, and with some coordinate elements within the
basically subordinate structure."[4] Hamilton also places Milton in a
continuum somewhere between Hooker and Browne. For Hooker, the
dispassionate expositor of truth, the perfectly ordered suspensions
of the Ciceronian period comprised a medium appropriate for com-
municating perfect, true ideas. Browne, on the other hand, was a
more playful Christian humanist, always alert for the odd circumstances he could loosely associate with the true ideas he took for
granted, for the most part the ideas Hooker had expounded. Milton
had his own definite ideas and purposes, Hamilton further argues, and
these were the ideas and purposes of a political crusader who ranged
widely in search of support for his points. The definite ideas require
complex suspensions; the wide-ranging search for support results in
some "loose components . . . and coordinate elements" (pp. 310–12).

In my opinion, Hamilton is correct to locate the source of Milton's
unique prose style in the fact that he was engaging in political rhetoric. I also find it useful to pursue further the relationship both he and

Williamson suggest between the styles of Milton, Browne, and Hooker. I shall analyze two passages by Milton along with two others, one by Browne and one by Hooker. Each is similar in subject to the corresponding passage by Milton, and each stylistically resembles but contrasts with it in ways characteristic enough to repay careful and extended comparison. Browne begins the Religio Medici with a long sentence defending his Christian orthodoxy and describing its origin and development:

> For my Religion, though there be severall circumstances that
> might perswade the world I have none at all, as the generall
> scandall of my profession, the naturall course of my studies, the
> indifferency of my behaviour, and discourse in matters of Religion,
> neither violently defending one, nor with that common ardour and
> contention opposing another; yet in despight hereof I dare, without
> usurpation, assume the honorable stile of a Christian: not that I
> meerely owe this title to the Font, my education, or Clime wherein
> I was borne, as being bred up either to confirme those principles
> my Parents instilled into my unwary understanding; or by a gen-
> erall consent proceed in the Religion of my Countrey: But having,
> in my riper yeares, and confirmed judgement, seene and examined
> all, I finde my selfe obliged by the principles of Grace, and the
> law of mine owne reason, to embrace no other name but this;
> neither doth herein my zeale so farre make me forget the generall
> charitie I owe unto humanity, as rather to hate then pity Turkes,
> Infidels, and (what is worse) Jewes, rather contenting my selfe to
> enjoy that happy stile, then maligning those who refuse so glorious
> a title.[5]

The primary structure of this sentence is a complex Ciceronian suspension: "though there be . . . yet in despight hereof I dare. . . ." This bare outline is assertive and oratorical, uncommonly so for Browne. He bravely confronts the aspersions often cast upon physicians and quietists, then surmounts them with a rhetorical flourish: "Yet in despight hereof I dare, without usurpation, assume the honorable stile of a Christian." However, in listing "the circumstances that might perswade the world" he has no religion at all, Browne attacks anti-intellectualism and religious intolerance in a subtler way. The third circumstance, "the indifferency of my behaviour, and discourse in matters of Religion," begets a pair of participial clauses, "neither violently defending one, nor with that common ardour and contention opposing another." These clauses are essential to neither the logical nor the rhetorical progress of the sentence; they are examples of one of the devices of the loose style enumerated by Croll, participial constructions which, noncommittal in relation to the rest of the sentence, contribute to a sense of spontaneous, unpremeditated thought (p. 221). Having arrived at the subject of religious behavior and discourse in developing his premeditated thought, Browne pauses and remembers the violent religious controversies of the 1630s. What appears to be gratuitous elaboration in fact expresses the humane and tolerant attitude that lay behind the traditional concept of "indifferency," the granting of liberty to Christians in matters of religion not essential to salvation. Browne thus comments with telling irony on the zealous and interminable controversies over just such indifferent matters. And he also comments on his own overzealous defense of himself, which he has been conducting in a suspended oratorical syntax he has momentarily forgotten. He begins the Religio by deploying the looseness of his style to display a charitable disposition, and this indicates the main idea of the entire sentence, the indispensability of charity to faith. One of the functions of the loose style throughout the Religio is to demonstrate the necessity of this relationship.

The unqualified, emphatic assertion of the main clause, "yet in despight hereof I dare . . . ," is weakened again by still further elaboration: "not that I meerely owe . . . ." On the other hand, this clause begins another emphatic suspended construction containing a more substantial self-defense: "not that I meerely owe . . . But having . . . I finde my selfe obliged by the principles of Grace, and the law of mine owne reason, to embrace no other name but this." Again between the introduction and resolution of the ostensible main idea falls a loose participial construction: "as being bred up . . . or by a generall consent proceed . . . ." And again this loosens up the apparently suspended structure of the sentence. The words, "the Font, my education, or Clime wherein I was borne," entice Browne into pausing and appreciating the entire process of nurture: "as being bred up either to confirme those principles my Parents instilled into my unwary understanding; or by a generall consent proceed in the Religion of my Countrey." The clause dissipates the simple rhetorical force of the strenuous antithesis, "not that . . . But," so that the mature Browne's religious convictions fulfill his upbringing rather than transcend it. This sense of interest in something for its own sake, to which the loose, rambling style is admirably suited, is a principal foundation of Browne's gentle, charitable disposition. Thus, after reiterating his declaration of faith in the second main clause ("I finde my selfe obliged . . . to embrace no other name but this"), Browne again elaborates, explicitly defining the terms of the counterpoint of styles I have been analyzing. The suspended oratorical style in which he has been battling the accusations of the "world" he calls "zeale." The looser, quieter style in which he has been commenting on all the par-

ticipants in this struggle he associates with "the generall charitie I
owe unto humanity" by appending another pair of participial clauses
which amount to a summary description of charitable religion:
"rather contenting my selfe to enjoy that happy stile, then maligning
those who refuse so glorious a title." One has the feeling that in this
introductory statement, Browne is defining his unique area and mode
of discourse, backing away from the Puritan-Anglican controversy
and divesting himself of the rhetorical zeal by which it was waged.
In the serene tone of these concluding participial clauses, he settles
comfortably into his private version of Christian humanism.[6]

In a sentence at the end of the personal digression in The Reason
of Church Government, Milton describes his upbringing and religious
attitudes in the course of justifying his participation in the ecclesiastical controversy Browne shunned:

> But were it the meanest under-service, if God by his Secretary
> conscience injoyn it, it were sad for me if I should draw back,
> for me especially, now when all men offer their aid to help ease
> and lighten the difficult labours of the Church, to whose service
> by the intentions of my parents and friends I was destin'd of a
> child, and in mine own resolutions, till comming to some ma-
> turity of yeers and perceaving what tyranny had invaded the
> Church, that he who would take Orders must subscribe slave,
> and take an oath withall, which unlesse he took with a conscience
> that would retch, he must either strait perjure, or split his faith,
> I thought it better to preferre a blamelesse silence before the
> sacred office of speaking bought, and begun with servitude and
> forswearing. [I:822-23]

As in the corresponding passage in Browne, the primary structure of
this sentence is Ciceronian and oratorical: "But were it . . . if God
. . . it were sad . . . ." In the two subordinate clauses, the idea passes
through steadily intensifying degrees of emphasis, "the meanest un-
der-service, . . . God by his Secretary conscience injoyn it," and is
resolved in the main clause by understatement. In this way Milton
avoids the note of bombast we found in Browne's affirmation of faith:
"it were sad for me if I should draw back . . . ." This understatement
is itself a device of emphasis; it repeats the form of the subordinate
clauses ("were it . . . if God . . . it were . . . if I . . ."), showing
energies not concentrated but dissipated, and thus emphasizing the
heroic quality of Christian vocation by contrast with its fugitive and
cloistered opposite. Milton then passes on to more obvious forms of
emphasis: "for me especially . . . ." The clause introduced by these
words is|an apposition, another of the features of the loose style enu-
merated by Croll. That is to say, Milton's and Browne's uses of the

loose style are diametrically opposed. Instead of questioning the zeal
of the suspended style, Milton's looseness reasserts it, enlarging the
scope of its concerns, here carrying it forward into the public domain:
"for me especially, now when all men offer their aid to help ease and
lighten the difficult labours of the Church." The word "Church" gives
Milton another opportunity to prolong, expand, and intensify the sentence: "to whose service by the intentions . . . ." This is the "trailing
effect" analyzed by Croll, in which a member is linked not to the general idea of the preceding member, but to its last word.[7] In Milton
this device is not designed as it is in Browne to lead the mind toward
delightful qualifying perceptions. Rather, it leads to a more public,
emphatic perception of the zealous imperatives that force Milton to
become a pamphleteer. With each "independent motion" of his mind,
Browne discovers something finer than zeal. Possessed of a mind
equally agile and vigorous, Milton discovers with each intellectual
gesture that zeal is all the more urgently demanded. And so this
trailing clause soon moves on to a more grandiose and comprehensive
suspension than the initial one: "till comming . . . and perceaving . . .
that he who . . . I thought . . . ." A secondary trailing effect occurs
within one of the subordinate members of this suspension; this in turn
produces a secondary suspension: "an oath withall, which unlesse he
. . . he must . . . ." Repeatedly, emotional energy is built up in the
suspended members and released into the emphatic main clauses.
Thus, in this second network of suspensions, Milton's repugnance for
the immoral impositions of the prelates is gradually intensified through
the successive subordinate members ("what tyranny . . . must sub-
scribe slave . . . a conscience that would retch . . . must either strait
perjure, or split his faith . . ."), then explosively resolved and rounded
off by a periodic return in the main clause: "I thought it better to pre-
ferre a blamelesse silence before the sacred office of speaking bought,
and begun with servitude and forswearing." By these involved com-
binations of the two learned styles available to him, Milton tries to
prove in as emphatic and compelling a way as possible that his upbringing was not fulfilled, as was Browne's, but rudely disrupted by
the intolerable state of public affairs.

   According to Croll, the Ciceronian period subsides at the end, after
having reached its most emphatic point somewhere near its center.
The loose period, on the other hand, becomes more vigorous and ex-
pansive as it proceeds, rising at the end to an oh altitudo (p. 228). We
have seen a quiet version of this in the period from the Religio analyzed above. Browne's mind continually veers toward the more con-
genial subject of charity. His oh altitudo consists in shifting the
perspective of discourse so that tensions are dissolved on a higher
plane. Milton uses an oh altitudo movement that combines loose in-

tellectual momentum with Ciceronian structure. His mind presses
forward to synthesize all the moral and political implications of an
issue and all the emotions they generate. The result is that the
reader is presented with a vivid narrative of Milton's religious
decisions and of the public crisis that necessitated them. In more
directly stylistic terms, Milton's mind moves from one suspended
sentence to a longer, more emphatic one. The links between these
rounded suspensions are usually the devices of the loose style. By
these means, Milton imparts a sense of urgency to his ceremonious,
Latinate public utterances. As distinguished from Browne, who suggests an absolute conflict between the quiet humanity of the loose
stylist and the noisy rhetoric which exacerbates public disputes,
Milton insists on the connections between private and public crises,
insists that the private energies implied by the loose style must
regenerate the dignified public institutions implied by Ciceronian
oratory.[8]

   Thus, Milton's special use of the loose style is explained by the
fact that he was a radical propagandist with allegiances to the tradition of Christian humanism. Conversely, his distinctive use of the
more structured, suspended style may be traced to the fact that he
meant to adapt Christian humanism to radical purposes. This ac-
counts for the differences between the characteristic rhythms of
his suspensions and those of Hooker. Both Hooker and Milton sub-
scribe to the doctrine that civil society was formed to protect man
against the consequences of the Fall. Hooker's version of this myth
is in Book I of the Polity:

   To take away all such mutual grievances, injuries, and wrongs,
   there was no way but only by growing unto composition and
   agreement amongst themselves, by ordaining some kind of government public, and by yielding themselves subject thereunto; that
   unto whom they granted authority to rule and govern, by them
   the peace, tranquillity, and happy estate of the rest might be procured. Men always knew that when force and injury was offered
   they might be defenders of themselves; they knew that howsoever
   men may seek their own commodity, yet if this were done with
   injury unto others it was not to be suffered, but by all men and by
   all good means to be withstood; finally they knew that no man
   might in reason take upon him to determine his own right, and
   according to his own determination proceed in maintenance thereof, inasmuch as every man is towards himself and them whom he
   greatly affecteth partial; and therefore that strifes and troubles
   would be endless, except they gave their common consent all to
   be ordered by some whom they should agree upon: without which

consent there were no reason that one man should take upon him
to be lord or judge over another; because, although there be according to the opinion of some very great and judicious men a
kind of natural right in the noble, wise, and virtuous, to govern
them which are of servile disposition; nevertheless for manifestation of this their right, and men's more peaceable contentment
on both sides, the assent of them who are to be governed seemeth
necessary.[9]

The suspensions of the first sentence show the unimpeded progress
of harmony and order in civil society. The first member introduces
this idea and begins to embody it in a triplet: "mutual grievances,
injuries, and wrongs." The key to the serene tone of the passage is
found at the start of the second member: "there was no way but only
. . . ." The passage is about making a virtue of necessity by knowing
how to submit to it. A dignified submission produces order, and so
the triple parallelism of the second member answers to the triplet of
the first, increasing the sense of harmonious resonance as it develops
the main idea of eliminating violent disorder by instituting government: "by growing unto composition . . . by ordaining . . . by yielding
themselves . . . ." The peaceful and prosperous life that civil society
makes possible is then both described and evoked in the balanced suspension and smooth rising and falling rhythm of the third member:
"that unto whom they granted authority to rule and govern, by them
the peace, tranquillity, and happy estate of the rest might be procured."[10] The form of this sentence, imaging the effortless emergence of social order, is appropriate for a work expounding the
innately harmonious tendencies of the entire universe. Once men
have submitted to necessity, a beneficent social order necessarily
follows. In the progressively richer constructions of the members
of this period, Hooker suggests that social conflict will be minimized
as soon as men attend to first principles. Of course, Hooker wrote
all of Book I to make just this point.

The second, longer sentence expounds these first principles more
systematically, serenely reinforcing the pervasive implication that
men must necessarily consent to be ruled by political authority. Each
member of the long parallel series ("Men always knew that . . . they
knew that . . . finally they knew that . . .") states a general principle
of social behavior which must be seen in conjunction with the other
members of the series. The sentence is a syllogism making explicit
what is implicit in the more artful construction of the first sentence.
Its formal completion by the final member of the parallel series thus
coincides with its logical conclusion, which turns consent of the governed into unavoidable constraint: "and therefore that strifes and
troubles would be endless, except they gave their common consent all

to be ordered by some whom they should agree upon . . . ." Finally,
in another series of suspensions, Hooker further dilutes the element
of free choice implicit in the idea of consent of the governed by using
it to uphold the general principle of human inequality and its consequence, social hierarchy. After apparently not committing himself
to this principle ("although there be according to the opinion of some
very great and judicious men . . ."), he makes it simply reappear in
his reaffirmation of the necessity for consent of the governed, as if
it were an inevitable feature of civil society, just as in the first sentence, peace and prosperity simply appeared as the inevitable results
of the social contract: "nevertheless for manifestation of this their
right, and men's more peaceable contentment on both sides, the assent
of them who are to be governed seemeth necessary." Hooker's Ciceronian style, then, the style of "an English Aristotle set to music,"[11]
does not describe the actions of free men. Rather, in both its subtly
rhetorical uses, as in the first sentence and the final part of the
second, and its more strictly logical uses, as in the first part of the
second sentence, it squares and measures human actions to the rules
of philosophical necessity. Proceeding through suspensions to logical or quasi-logical resolutions, philosophical necessity moves on
its serene way to the conclusion that the social contract and a hierarchical society are inseparable. Hooker's style imposes a necessary
form on history.

Milton's version of this myth appears in The Tenure of Kings and
Magistrates:

No man who knows ought, can be so stupid to deny that all men
naturally were borne free, being the image and resemblance of
God himself, and were by privilege above all the creatures, born
to command and not to obey: and that they liv'd so. Till from the
root of Adams transgression, falling among themselves to doe
wrong and violence, and foreseeing that such courses must needs
tend to the destruction of them all, they agreed by common league
to bind each other from mutual injury, and joyntly to defend themselves against any that gave disturbance or opposition to such
agreement . . . . And because no faith in all was found sufficiently
binding, they saw it needfull to ordaine som authoritie, that might
restrain by force and punishment what was violated against peace
and common right. This autoritie and power of self-defence and
preservation being originally and naturally in every one of them,
and unitedly in them all, for ease, for order, and least each man
should be his own partial Judge, they communicated and deriv'd
either to one, whom for the eminence of his wisdom and integritie
they chose above the rest, or to more then one whom they thought
of equal deserving: the first was call'd a King; the other Magis-

trates. Not to be thir Lords and Maisters (though afterward those
names in som places were giv'n voluntarily to such as had been
Authors of inestimable good to the people) but, to be thir Deputies
and Commissioners, to execute, by vertue of thir intrusted power,
that justice which else every man by the bond of nature and of
Cov'nant must have executed for himself, and for one another.
[III:198–99]

As we saw, Hooker's Christian humanism focuses on the necessity
for a harmonious social order in a fallen world. The basis of Milton's
approach to the origins of society, and of his Christian humanism, is
contained in the phrase, "all men naturally were borne free." The
decision to constitute a social order he sees as a prudent measure by
which men retain as much freedom as possible in a fallen world. The
difference, and it makes all the difference, is one of emphasis. In
Hooker the accent is on orderly submission to necessity, in Milton,
on constructive actions that are necessary. The texture of Milton's
passage is thus sharp and vigorous rather than calm and serene.
Milton's constructions are governed by active verbs and verbals,
Hooker's by passive and intransitive forms: "foreseeing . . . they
agreed . . . to bind . . . and joyntly to defend . . . they saw it needfull
. . . they communicated and deriv'd . . . to execute . . ." as opposed
to "there was no way . . . might be procured . . . was offered . . .
might be defenders . . . if this were done . . . not to be suffered . . .
but . . . to be withstood . . . would be endless . . . seemeth necessary."
Hooker analyzes the conditions that limit the political will; Milton nar-
rates its dignified exercise. And it is significant that the two major
clauses in Milton's passage governed by the intransitive "to be" are
these: "This autoritie and power of self-defence and preservation
being originally and naturally in every one of them, and unitedly in
them all . . . Not to be thir Lords and Maisters . . . but, to be thir
Deputies and Commissioners." That is to say, at the beginning and
end of the passage, Milton emphasizes the only condition that interests
him, that "all men naturally were borne free" and that civil society
preserves this freedom.
    To a similar effect, Hooker's suspended periods move at a much
more leisurely pace than do Milton's. Each of Hooker's clauses is an
independent appreciation of the innate order of things: "they knew
that howsoever men may seek their own commodity, yet if this were
done with injury unto others it was not to be suffered, but by all men
and by all good means to be withstood." In these unobtrusive rising
and falling rhythms, conflict itself becomes a harmonious readjust-
ment of energies. When this sentence is completed, therefore, its
conclusion simply falls into place as the explicit fulfillment of these
many preliminary glimpses of universal harmony. Hooker is not dis-

cussing the social contract so much as he is relating it to a larger
pattern, and this of course is the general method of the Polity. Issues, in particular the issue of church government, lose their specific impact as they are absorbed into this larger harmonious pattern.
It is precisely such specific impact, on the other hand, which Milton
wishes to preserve and intensify, here the specific nature of the
social contract as an exercise in civil prudence by which men surrender lawless license in order to retain lawful liberty. Thus the
sentences move briskly toward the active verbs listed above. In the
second and fourth sentences quoted, the suspended Ciceronian syntax
enacts a pattern in which right reason perceives and analyzes a
political problem and active virtue vigorously resolves it: "falling
among themselves . . . foreseeing that such courses must needs . . .
they agreed . . . to bind each other . . . and joyntly to defend . . . for
ease, for order, and least each man should be his own partial Judge,
they communicated and deriv'd . . . whom for the eminence of his
wisdom and integritie they chose."[12] The two intransitive clauses
discussed above amount to more explicit affirmations of freedom and
dignity and substantiate the virtù of these original political acts. They
also keep to the forefront of the discussion the major polemical thesis
of the Tenure, implicit in the active texture of the entire passage, that
government depends on the active support of the governed, which may
be revoked when the conditions of support are not fulfilled. In Hooker's leisurely syntactical movement is a suggestion that vigorous
action is more than likely to be indecorous and disorderly. Milton's
more rapid, energetic, and emphatic pace asserts that disorder cannot be controlled except by vigorous action.

Milton and Popular Prose Styles

The fact is, however, that Milton's contemporaries paid little attention to his political activities. The tracts in English remained unread
or misunderstood, and Milton got a name for himself during his life-
time only when the learned community of Europe started talking from
side to side about his Latin Defences.[13] In part because of the literary
origins of his political commitments, Milton was outside the political
mainstream throughout his political life, sometimes in his subject
matter, sometimes in his sense of rhetorical occasion, always in his
manner of writing. He could appeal to connoisseurs of Latin polemics
and he appeals now to literary critics who would like to share his faith
in the political significance of imagination, but he was not heard, apparently, by most of the men of seventeenth-century England who had
committed themselves, as he had, to fundamental alterations in church
and state. It is worth considering whether or not the way Milton writes
has anything to do with his remarkable lack of political success. The

preceding section attempts to define some of the imaginative virtues
of Milton's political prose. In this section I want to explore some of
the limitations of that prose as a medium of political action. According to William Haller, the most successful political agitators of the
Puritan Revolution were the Leveller leaders. Powerless otherwise,
they created a mass following and an organized political party almost
solely by means of skillful propaganda.[14] Thus, if Milton's prose can
be put to a literary test by comparing it with that of Hooker and
Browne, comparing it with that of John Lilburne and William Walwyn
will constitute a test of its immediate political effectiveness.

During one of his many indefinite sojourns in prison, this one imposed in 1649 by the Council of State on which Milton served as Latin
secretary,[15] Lilburne composed The Legall Fundamental Liberties
of the People of England. A good deal of this tract is occupied with
an autobiographical self-defense against the charge that Lilburne is
a madly contentious figure, endlessly and gratuitously picking fights
with those in authority. Lilburne's reply must be quoted at length to
be appreciated:

Well, in the next place the Wars begun betwixt them and the
King; and truly having seriously read all their primitive most
excellent Declarations, and sufficiently my self smarted under
the Kings irregular government, in the violating of the Laws of
England, the compact betwixt him and his people; . . . and reading
in the Scripture, Rom. 13. that the end of the institution of all
Magistracy in the world, is for a terror to evill doers, and for a
praise to those that doe well; the serious consideration of which,
wrought out something in reason in my own thoughts, to ballance
the letter of those Laws, (which I then knew were absolutely for
the King) somthing like those generall rules or maximes in Law,
recorded by that most excellent of English Lawyers, Sir Edw.
Cook, in his 4 part. Institut. fol. 330. which are, That although
the Law (of England) speak in generall terms, yet it is to be bound
up, or accepted, but where reason ceaseth, there the law ceaseth;
for seeing reason is the very life and spirit of the Law it self, the
Lawgiver is not to be esteemed to respect that which hath no reason, although the generality of the words at the first sight, or after
the Letter seem otherwise: And it, in my reason, could not be
rationall for any men to appoint a compact to be betwixt two parties, but to bind both equally alike, King as well as people; and not
to keep the people bound to the expresse letter of the Kings part,
or any others, when the King or that other, shall break his or
theirs in twenty particulars, as by Shipmoney, Projects, &c. And
further, saith Cook, fol. 328. ibid. . . . So upon these or the like

grounds, I took up arms in judgment and conscience against the
King, . . . till Manchester visibly degenerated, and would have
hanged me, for being over-honest, and over active in taking in
Tikel Castle too soon: which with his visible turning knave, and
apparently betraying his trust at Dennington, in designing his
Army, or the best part of it, a sacrifice to the Kings fury, made
me engage against him and others of his Associates, with Crom-
wel, who thereunto sollicited me, and also threw up my Commis-
sion; and so his basenesse spoyled a Souldier of me, that I could
never fight as a Souldier since; . . . But no sooner was I by the
ears with Manchester, who first began with me, but Mr Prynn
wrote his desperate invective Books against us all that would not
be conformable to the Covenant (that Cheat,) and the Scots Pres-
bytery (that every thing and nothing;) and would have had us all
destroyed, or banished the Land of our Nativity: so in conscience
to God, and safety to my self and brethren (Mr Edmund Roser, my
present unworthy Antagonist, being then my pastor or teacher) I
was inwardly compelled to deal with him, that thus sought to destroy the generation of the righteous; and accordingly I wrote him
a sharp Epistle, now in print, dated 7 Jan. 1644. which brought
upon my back a whole sea of troubles; and a Vote or Votes in the
House of Commons past against me: whereupon, without any more
adoe, black Corbet and the Committee of Examinations makes me
a Prisoner, and tosseth and tumbleth me to the purpose: So before
him, upon the 13 of June 1645, was I forced to give in my reasons
(now in print) wherefore I wrote that excellent and seasonable
Epistle (which was the first avowed publick Cannon I know of in
England, discharged against the then insulting Presbyter, for the
liberty of the consciences of my present bloudy and malicious
persecutors, that now stile themselves the Pastours and Leaders
of the Churches of God; but do indeed and in truth, by their unnat-
urall, unchristian, and unjust actions deserve no other stile, but
men fit for nothing but to be the Pastors and Leaders of the Synagogue of Satan.) The whole story of which contest with Mr Prynn,
you may read at large in the beginning of my Book, called Inno-
cency and Truth justified. . . .

   And then before I well got rid of this broyl, you your self
[William Lenthall, Speaker of the Commons, to whom the tract is
addressed] got the House of Commons the 19 day of July 1645. to
fall upon my bones, and Vote me to prison I know not wherefore,
unlesse it were for riding post from Summerset-shire through
twenty dangers to bring you the first news of the Lord Gorings
Army being routed at Lampert.[16]

Superficially, this passage resembles a type we will encounter repeatedly in Milton's writings. An extended series of participial clauses, each of which can sprout any number of interpolated members, builds to a climax in a major predication: "So upon these or the like grounds, I took up arms in judgment and conscience against the King." The rhetorical energy thereby accumulated and released then spills over and produces an open-ended series of coordinate members. If one attends only to this apparent syntax, the effect is the same as in Milton: Lilburne deals his opponents a crushing blow by encompassing or containing them within an elaborate structure of principled utterance. The shape of the sentence implies the shape of a reformed society, and the density and repetitious emphasis of the sentence imply the massive inertial resistance of the status quo. Struggling for liberty with the pen is made to seem no less heroic than waging war for it with the sword.

Despite this overall structure, however, and despite the other ways in which Lilburne suggests the seriousness of the threat posed by the unjust party, such as his near-pedantic citation of authorities and of his own previous books, I find that the passage substantiates Joan Webber's claim that Lilburne's prose does not build towards climaxes but is primarily characterized by a sense of free flow.[17] Lilburne writes far more loosely than Browne or even Montaigne. Throughout he employs only the most perfunctory and neutral kinds of coordinate transitions. Even within the subordinate clauses at the beginning of the passage, in which Lilburne is presumably orchestrating all the things that justify his asserting that he "took up arms in judgment and conscience against the King," the rhythm of construction is so often interrupted by the asides which contain the main matter that it completely disappears: "and reading in the Scripture . . . the serious consideration of which . . . those generall rules or maximes in Law . . . which are, That although . . . for seeing reason is . . . And it, in my reason, could not be rationall . . . in twenty particulars, as by Shipmoney, Projects, &c. And further, saith Cook, fol. 328. ibid."

One effect of this absolutely loose and chatty manner is that the first person character comes across as a tireless fighter for justice, tireless because the absence of full stops creates an impression that there is no relief from the swift flow of injustice: "But no sooner was I by the ears with Manchester, who first began with me, but Mr Prynn wrote his desperate invective Books . . . And then before I well got rid of this broyl, you your self got the House of Commons the 19 day of July 1645. to fall upon my bones." The organization of the passage makes the point, and the shapeless syntax reinforces it, that Lilburne and the liberties he represents are not to be silenced or suppressed, no matter how often he may be arbitrarily and cruelly treated. Above

all else, though, this style is antiheroic. Its lack of structure is a
commentary on any reformer or reforming party, Presbyterian,
Independent, or Milton's heroic poet, who would coerce society to fit
a preconceived pattern. Lilburne's world is the real world of seventeenth-century political turmoil, richly circumstantial, with times,
places, and dramatis personae always carefully specified, and Lilburne's political life flows entirely on this genuine level. He denies
himself the heroic voice and levels unnecessary and overrefined
subordinations in discourse as he would level them in society, to the
point of abolishing the subordinate relationship between followers
and leader. The shape of the reformed society is to be generated by
the entire community from the disorderly welter of particulars which
comprise real experience, not by self-appointed heroes from their
own minds. Lilburne's prose is egalitarian almost to the point of
anarchy.[18]

No man, in other words, can presume to fabricate the one true order under which his fellows must live and according to which they
must think, speak, and write. The best that can be done in such a
fluid and uncertain situation is to keep reasserting the fundamental
principles from which all genuine political order must derive, and
the importance of this task can be further emphasized by enunciating
such principles at points which are the most unlikely and disruptive
syntactically but perhaps the most appropriate and effective rhetorically: "wherefore I wrote that excellent and seasonable Epistle (which
was the first avowed publick Cannon I know of in England, discharged
against the then insulting Presbyter, for the liberty of the consciences
of my present bloudy and malicious persecutors, that now stile themselves the Pastours and Leaders of the Churches of God; but do indeed
and in truth, by their unnatural, unchristian, and unjust actions deserve
no other stile, but men fit for nothing but to be the Pastors and Leaders
of the Synagogue of Satan)." With this typical parenthesis, Lilburne
accomplishes the major purpose of his tract, to show that while his
narrative is the story of unjust suffering at the hands of arbitrary
power, it is also the story of the enduring strength of liberty and of
men who know themselves to be free. Like this aside emerging from
the flux of narration, freedom and free men remain alive and well,
capable of maintaining a loose, provisional, and generalized control of
political events. If Lilburne must do endless battle with a succession
of turncoats from the cause of true liberty, from Bastwick and Prynne
to Cromwell and the Independent ministers, these backsliding oppres-
sors simply give him renewed opportunities to demonstrate that he
remains free and vigorous. Lilburne's prose style would have us believe that any man of sound sense and firm conviction can do anything
a presumed reformer can do without the stylistic posturing which contradicts the reformer's alleged goals.

In his Apology, Milton defends himself at length against the Modest
Confuter's flimsy accusations of licentiousness with his well-known
account of his literary, philosophical, and religious education. The
following passage brings to conclusion and climax the story of his
nurturing in the classics:

> Thus from the Laureat fraternity of Poets, riper yeares, and the
> ceaselesse round of study and reading led me to the shady spaces
> of philosophy, but chiefly to the divine volumes of Plato, and his
> equall Xenophon. Where if I should tell ye what I learnt, of chas-
> tity and love, I meane that which is truly so, whose charming cup
> is only vertue which she bears in her hand to those who are worthy.
> The rest are cheated with a thick intoxicating potion which a cer-
> taine Sorceresse the abuser of loves name carries about; and how
> the first and chiefest office of love, begins and ends in the soule,
> producing those happy twins of her divine generation knowledge and
> vertue, with such abstracted sublimities as these, it might be worth
> your listning, Readers, as I may one day hope to have ye in a still
> time, when there shall be no chiding; not in these noises, the ad-
> versary as ye know, barking at the doore; or searching for me at
> the Burdello's where it may be he has lost himselfe, and raps up
> without pitty the sage and rheumatick old Prelatesse with all her
> young Corinthian Laity to inquire for such a one. [I:891–92]

Here Milton is truly using the sentence structure Lilburne appeared
to be using in the passage discussed above. The major sentence builds
through the series of coyly conditional clauses and reaches a climax
in the resolving clause, "with such abstracted sublimities as these, it
might be worth your listning, Readers, as I may one day hope to have
ye in a still time, when there shall be no chiding." Except for the
portion reminiscent of Comus ("The rest . . . carries about . . ."),
the sentence does not confront and absorb hostile forces or ideas as
part of its ascending movement. It is unusually calm and serene for
Milton's prose, as is the entire autobiographical digression. As
Webber remarks, the periodic sentences of these autobiographical
passages are prose poetry, tantalizing intimations both in subject and
style of the kind of thing Milton expects to achieve once the revolution
is consummated (p. 202). For our purposes, however, the most interesting aspect of the passage is its tail or afterthought. After rising to
his earnest and sincere expression of his hope for the withering away
of politics, for that "still time, when there shall be no chiding," Milton
remembers the Confuter and all he represents: "not in these noises,
the adversary as ye know, barking at the doore; or searching for me
at the Burdello's where it may be he has lost himselfe, and raps up
without pitty the sage and rheumatick old Prelatesse with all her young

Corinthian Laity to inquire for such a one." Artfully and I believe deliberately, Milton portrays the political struggle in which he is engaged as a distraction, an anticlimactic nuisance. He has led the reader into the chaste and pure air of literary and philosophical idealism, and of the reformed society Milton believes to be identical with this intellectual's paradise. From this perspective political issues appear trivial and can be easily disposed of with an urbane flourish.

It is not too extravagent to claim that the construction of this sentence reveals Milton's fundamental limitations as a political activist. We remember that Lilburne, by his avoidance of stylistic climaxes, enforces the sense that political struggles do not readily yield ideal resolutions. By his habit of specifying everything, he creates an impression of social and political reality and of his own readiness to dwell and thrive in the midst of turmoil. By his repeated and apparently haphazard digressions into discussions of principle, he makes us believe that principles can not only survive but flourish when applied to and tested against actual life. But Milton yearns for the climax, the still time which is the consummation of the sentence and would be the consummation of these unpleasant political broils and of his literary ambitions. His curiously hesitant format ("Where if I should tell ye what I learnt . . .)" makes him appear almost precious or demure, fearful lest his cherished principles become sullied by contact with political contentions. And the "abstracted sublimity" of the sentence combined with the trailing glance at the Confuter suggest that for Milton the goal is not insuring that principles will survive within actual life and support it, but rather establishing an ideal realm to which actual life must conform or be dismissed as worthless. For the time being, it is true, Milton does genuinely believe that social reality will eventually prove equal to his idealistic demands, that in the not too distant future self-revelation and idealistic discourse will not be a digression, as he pretends it is within this sentence and within the tract at large, but the main substance of human living together. It seems to me, however, that by his near-literal belief that the truest index of genuine reformation would be society's ability to appreciate his poems, Milton guarantees political disappointment and bitterness for himself. As a medium of political persuasion, Lilburne's prose is both more realistic and more broadly appealing.

Since it may seem unfair to compare the utterances of an experienced political leader with those of a relative novice, I will now discuss a passage from the Tenure, which appeared early in 1649 shortly after the execution of Charles I, in conjunction with one from a tract called The Bloody Project, which was published in August 1648 and

was almost certainly written by William Walwyn. After analyzing
the behavior of each of the parties to the increasingly fragmented
Puritan coalition and demonstrating that each has shown itself to be
motivated entirely by factional self-interest, Walwyn summarizes
the impasse to which these narrow maneuvers have brought the English polity:

> To be short, all the quarrell we have at this day in the King-
> dome, is no other then a quarrel of Interests, and Partyes, a
> pulling down of one Tyrant, to set up another, and instead of
> Liberty, heaping upon our selves a greater slavery then that we
> fought against: certainly this is the Liberty that is so much
> strove for, and for which there are such fresh endeavours to
> engage men; but if you have not killed and destroyed men enough
> for this, go on and destroy, kill and sley, till your consciences
> are swoln so full with the blood of the People, that they burst
> agen, and upon your death-beds may you see your selves the
> most horrid Murtherers that ever lived, since the time that Cain
> kild his brother without a just Cause; for where, or what is your
> cause? Beleeve it yee have a heavy reeckoning to make, and must
> undergo a sad repentance, or it will go ill with you at the great
> day, when all the sophistry of your great Reformers will serve
> you to little purpose, every man for himselfe being to give an
> account for the things which he hath done in the body, whether
> they be good or evill: Then it will serve you to little purpose
> to say, the King, Parliament, Army, Independents, Presbyterians,
> such an Officer, Magistrate, or Minister deluded me; no more
> then it did Adam, to say the woman whom thou gavest, &c. It
> being thus decreed in heaven, the soule which sinneth shall sure-
> ly dye.19

In a manner precisely the opposite of Lilburne's, Walwyn asserts that
all who have held power since 1641 have deserted the cause of justice
and liberty. Lilburne generates a sense of realism through the abundance of particulars he provides, Walwyn through the curt lucidity of
a man who knows how to interpret what is going on. To a reader of
the rhetoric of the "well-affected party," including a reader of Milton,
the first sentence of this passage comes as a blessed relief: "To be
short, all the quarrell we have at this day in the Kingdome, is no
other then a quarrel of Interests, and Partyes, a pulling down of one
Tyrant, to set up another." Amidst reams of high-minded obfusca-
tion, a writer who in sober good sense calls things by their right
names ("quarrel of Interests, and Partyes") can pass for a wit,
especially when he goes on to encompass the confused political situation in an apt formula, "a pulling down of one Tyrant, to set up
another."

The speaker thus begins as the voice of cool and composed reason, detaching himself from political reality that he may comment on it from a superior perspective, repeating his basic assertion and varying it just enough to avoid single- or simple-mindedness but not so much that he appears to be striving for literary elegance at the expense of what he, wants to communicate. He remains composed, but not quite so cool in the rest of the passage. Securely ensconced in his principled perspective, he addresses the soldiers and other common people who have enlisted in the service of one or another of these selfish parties with the commonplaces of popular preaching: deathbed, Judgment Day, the clearest and most elemental of scriptural myths. Here the sentences become longer, more elaborate, and more impassioned, without losing their clarity and homely vivacity. He speaks more warmly because he is speaking not to the would-be tyrants, but to all those who ought to know better. Those engaged in power plays are not to be taken as seriously as the masses of the people who allow such injustices to be perpetrated. In the second half of the passage, therefore, Walwyn begins to encompass the puny world of Interests and Parties in the superior perspective of justice and Judgment. Phrases such as "all the sophistry of your great Reformers," and "the King, Parliament, Army, Independents, Presbyterians, such an Officer, Magistrate, or Minister" are enclosed between predictions of inevitability ("yee have . . . must undergo . . .") and participial clauses which convey the certainty of settled truths: "every man for himselfe being to give an account . . . It being thus decreed in heaven . . . ." The people are informed that their leaders and deluders are trivial and weak creatures if they the people would only assert their own awesome power as Walwyn entreats them to do and as he himself succeeds in doing in the style of this passage. He thus challenges his audience to live up to those ideals in which they all profess to believe and for which they falsely imagine they have been fighting. But the audience is also invited to adopt this high-minded perspective and live by it, because the principles being invoked are universally accredited, because the repetition of such phrases as "will serve you to little purpose" helps make the passage clear and easy to follow, and because Walwyn speaks directly to that audience, with firmness, but also with familiarity and insight. The development of the passage, from sober and trenchant dispersal of mystification to warm but still lucid exhortation, amounts virtually to a "whisper in the ear" of Mr. John Milton, quietly advising him to ground his idealism and zeal in careful and sensible assessments of political reality.

Writing a few months later in defense of tyrannicide, Milton professes to find in the New Model Army and their Independent allies the party that stood resolute on principle when all others proved weak or selfish:

If God and a good cause give them Victory, the prosecution
wherof for the most part, inevitably draws after it the alteration
of Lawes, change of Goverment, downfal of Princes with thir
families; then comes the task to those Worthies which are the
soule of that enterprize, to be swett and labour'd out amidst the
throng and noises of Vulgar and irrational men. Some contesting
for privileges, customs, forms, and that old entanglement of
Iniquity, thir gibrish Lawes, though the badge of thir ancient
slavery. Others who have beene fiercest against thir Prince,
under the notion of a Tyrant, and no mean incendiaries of the
Warr against him, when God out of his providence and high dis-
posal hath deliver'd him into the hand of thir brethren, on a suddain and in a new garbe of Allegiance, which thir doings have
long since cancell'd; they plead for him, pity him, extoll him,
protest against those that talk of bringing him to the tryal of
Justice, which is the Sword of God, superior to all mortal things,
in whose hand soever by apparent signes his testified will is to
put it. [III:192–93]

In contrast to the passage from the Apology previously discussed,
Milton here creates an image of commitment to political struggle,
but it is an image entirely consistent with the loftiness of that earlier passage. Ideals are to be imposed on the English nation from
the top down, as "those Worthies which are the soule of that enterprize" labor to clear away the debris of custom, tradition, and
Presbyterian malignity and as God towers over the passage at the
beginning, middle, and end. The syntactical rhythm of the passage
underscores the feeling of heroic struggle proclaimed in the words
"the throng and noises of Vulgar and irrational men." The arrival
of the "still time, when there shall be no chiding" appears more
doubtful than it had in 1642. Thus, in the initial subordinate construction, "those Worthies" transcend the first set of obstacles to
revolutionary fulfillment, those listed in the "wherof" clause, only
to be confronted with the vulgar and irrational throng. Part of this
throng is curtly and contemptuously dismissed in the first participial clause, "Some contesting . . . ," but the revolutionary heroes
must again immediately contend with "Others" who are more powerful and dangerous and therefore must be dealt with by the more
strenuous means of a subsidiary subordinate construction: "Others
who have beene . . . when God out of his providence . . . on a suddain
. . . which thir doings . . . they plead for him . . . ." The interpolated relative pronoun clauses within this construction seek to dis-
able this perversity of the unnamed Presbyterians ("which thir
doings have long since cancell'd"), but it is as if the Presbyterian
forces had achieved a kind of demonically heroic momentum which

enables them to emerge triumphant in the second major predication:
"they plead for him, pity him, extoll him, protest against those that
talk of bringing him to the tryal of Justice." This momentum is to
be arrested by the concluding relative pronoun clause, "which is the
Sword of God . . . ," as though the revolutionary forces can only be
sustained by hurriedly throwing the divine sanction into the fray at
every juncture.

In Walwyn's passage, in other words, Christian truths function to
remind all men of their ordinary duties and to help insure a victory
for simple and commonplace justice. Milton pretends that Armaged-
don has come, that even though the issue is in doubt, God is supporting his worthies at every turn. Like Lilburne, Walwyn is both more
realistic and down to earth and more broadly appealing than Milton.
Walwyn names the enemies and thus gives them human credibility.
Milton loads them with epithets, turning them into demons. Walwyn
speaks directly to an audience, endowing his readers with potential
human strengths while exposing their weaknesses. He even human-
izes divinity, bringing it to bear on the individual fate of every
reader. Milton's God consists of remote and abstract categories,
providence and justice, and Milton appears not to be speaking to any
audience. His is the impersonal voice of wrath, not needing to substantiate his assertions about divine providence and justice with
scriptural citations, as does Walwyn, but simply thundering from his
idealistic mountaintop, crying woe and destruction on the reprobates
in the plain beneath. Indeed, Milton appears to be able to speak directly to other human beings only when he is espousing lofty ideals
in a positive way, as in autobiographical passages such as the one
discussed above or in Areopagitica. We have here, then, not political discourse or persuasion, not even political polemic, but a kind
of millennial melodrama. Instead of making a public statement,
Milton transforms the real configuration of political forces in 1649
into an image of his private longing for the ultimately redeeming
gestures of superhuman heroes.

Milton in the Idealistic Revolution

Although both Hooker and Browne use their respective styles to
minimize the desirability of participating in politics and although
Milton uses the same two styles to stress both its necessity and
urgency, comparing Milton with writers more deeply political and
comprehensively radical shows that Milton was fundamentally impatient with political activity. On one level, by joining Ciceronian
and anti-Ciceronian syntax, Milton's rhetoric reflects his notion of
a society both rooted in the tradition of Christian humanism and
renewed by energetic radical reform. But on another level, this

rhetoric is no more and no less than a personal and private testament. In the remainder of the present study, I will be tracing the ways in which Milton adapted his prose style and his rarefied political sensibility in response to the major events and developments of the English Revolution, but before undertaking this investigation in detail, I wish to notice briefly the close parallel—approaching identity—between the way Milton's idealism developed during his years of political activity and the broad historical pattern of those same revolutionary years.

Christopher Hill has argued persuasively that the Revolution was primarily a dispute within the ruling class.[20] During 1641–47, that is, during the two civil wars, the section of the ruling class that forced through such innovations as the New Model Army and eventually found its leader in Cromwell waged a militant struggle against the king and those elements in the ruling class that remained loyal to him. Cromwell and the other Independent leaders solicited the active support of many lower middle-class tradesmen and artisans who tended also to belong to radical religious sects. This willingness on the part of the Independents to mobilize a broader and less respectable following was what primarily distinguished them from their Presbyterian comrades in terms of revolutionary strategy. From the Presbyterian point of view, the Independent reliance on lower-class radicals was extremely dangerous. It threatened to make of the revolution not a responsible transfer of power to the "saints" among the ruling class, but a liberation of those who had heretofore "existed only to be ruled." Both the content and style of Milton's early pamphlets develop in a similar manner: Milton argues initially in the antiprelatical tracts only for the assumption of power by the saintly Presbyterian section of the ruling class. But his principled position is thrust towards increasingly radical applications by the energy of his style and thought, and in Areopagitica this tendency is combined with the assumption that the pamphlet articulates a broad national consensus for intellectual liberation. Milton presumes in his prose, as the ruling-class leaders of the Revolution did in reality, to orchestrate and control the behavior of newly awakened social groups.

During 1647–49, the tensions between the idealistic and propertied Independent revolutionary vanguard and their radical followers turned into open disagreements and conflicts. These were most dramatically expressed in the famous exchange between the Leveller agitator, Major Rainborough, and Cromwell's son-in-law, Henry Ireton, during the Army debates at Putney:

> Rainborough: For really I think that the poorest he that is in England hath a life to live, as the greatest he; and therefore

truly, sir, I think it's clear, that every man that is to live under a
government ought first by his own consent to put himself under
that government; and I do think that the poorest man in England is
not at all bound in a strict sense to that government that he hath
not had a voice to put himself under . . . .
    Ireton: But that by a man's being born here he shall have a
share in that power that shall dispose of the lands here, and of all
things here, I do not think it a sufficient ground. I am sure if we
look upon that which is the utmost . . . of what was originally the
constitution of this kingdom, upon that which is most radical and
fundamental, and which if you take away, there is no man hath any
land, any goods, or any civil interest, that is this: that those that
choose the representers for the making of laws by which this
state and kingdom are to be governed, are the persons who, taken
together, do comprehend the local interest of this kingdom; that
is, the persons in whom all land lies, and those in corporations
in whom all trading lies.[21]

In the sense in which I have been using the term, the Levellers and,
more resolutely, the "true Levellers" or Diggers led by Gerrard
Winstanley were not as idealistic as were the Independent Grandees
for whom Ireton spoke. Hill describes Cromwell, for example, as
combining "some genuinely radical religious beliefs with the normal
social assumptions of a country gentleman."[22] And Cromwell stood
firm throughout the Interregnum in enforcing a policy of religious
toleration against the wishes of Parliament. But being a country
gentleman, a man of property and substance, Cromwell also took
steps to prevent many of the material implications of this toleration
from becoming material realities. Men were left free to discuss
theology and to devise their own versions of doctrine and discipline,
but they were not allowed to discuss changes in, say, the hierarchical structure of property relations, much less to organize and act
upon the conclusions of such discussions. The toleration instituted
during the Interregnum was idealistic in that it made the ideal of
liberty of conscience into a social reality; yet it isolated that partially realized ideal from its full range of potential interactions with
the broad social and political context. The Leveller position enun-
ciated by Rainborough was less idealistic because it meant allowing
an idea like liberty of conscience to become more completely embodied, more truly present within "the world's body." In Winstanley's
words, "True freedom lies where a man receives his nourishment
and preservation, and that is in the use of the earth."
    What the Grandees' idealism meant in practice during the 1650s,
moreover, was the political isolation of the revolutionary governments. By executing the king, the Grandees alienated the rest of

the traditional ruling class, including their Presbyterian allies. By refusing to implement the Leveller program and by arresting the Leveller leaders, they alienated those lower-class and radical groups that had provided the main fighting strength of their victorious New Model Army. The Commonwealth and Protectorate regimes were thus left without any base of support in the wider community, and they had no alternative but to attempt to impose their ideals of toleration, education, and virtuous conduct on a hostile or, at best, indifferent nation. In sum, when the Revolution disavowed its own left wing in 1649 just after it had provided the counterrevolutionary right wing with a royal martyr, it set in motion a political dynamic that led logically to the Restoration.

Milton became the official apologist for the Revolution just when it cut itself off from its sources of support and turned conservative, so it is perhaps not surprising that his later prose, from the Tenure to The Readie and Easie Way, moves towards a relationship between speaker and audience which differs little from that between rulers and ruled during the Commonwealth and Protectorate. Although Milton would not have agreed with my analysis of the politics of the 1650s, he was certainly aware of the isolation of the revolutionary governments he served. He had only to compare the vast popularity of Eikon Basilike with the indifferent reception accorded Eikonoklastes.[23] Just as the governments of the 1650s forced innovations on a nation which had little use for them in the spiritualized forms those governments made them take, so Milton in his later pamphlets uses either a highly formal style to propose an increasingly abstracted ideal of pure social reason, or he uses a style marked by extremely loosened syntax to indicate more explicitly how imaginary this ideal has become in a nation heading rapidly towards the misrule of unreason. Both styles assume, in effect, that an audience for Milton's revolutionary ideals no longer exists and that it would be futile, if not demeaning, to try to recreate such an audience. These antirhetorical and therefore antipolitical ways of writing come to fruition as the medium of the gallant last stand Milton staged for himself by publishing the second edition of The Readie and Easie Way only weeks before the Restoration; such contempt for political reality is the logical culmination of Milton's political life.

2

THE ANTIPRELATICAL TRACTS

"Of Reformation Touching Church-Discipline in England"

With the publication of his first tract in May 1641, Milton embarked
on the "troubl'd sea of noises and hoars disputes," joining forces with
his boyhood tutor, Thomas Young, and the other Smectymnuuans
against Bishop Hall. A recent editor has praised the style of the antiprelatical tracts in the most fulsome terms: "Milton's attacks on the
bishops manifest the qualities that make his prose so great: an ex-
ploitation of the full resources of English from the poetic to the sub-
literary; striking images; concise, powerful, often highly sensuous
phrases; packed, sprawling sentences."[1] Of Reformation, however,
espouses the straight Presbyterian party line, and in it Milton's
vigorous style therefore serves a purpose common to all such parti-
san effusions: manipulating and exacerbating the zealous emotions of
the faithful. It is only fair to add that given the terms of the debate,
Milton's work could scarcely be more rational than it is. Bishop Hall
contended for the divine origin of episcopacy; the Smectymnuuans re-
plied that the Presbyterian discipline was clearly commanded in
Scripture. In Arthur E. Barker's words, "Conducted in these terms,
the argument reduces itself to the blank opposing of biblical interpretations and the citation of a cloud of patristic witnesses."[2] Even
these narrow grounds for rational maneuver are destroyed when
Milton simply assumes the truth of the Presbyterian argument and
devotes himself to condemning the "carnal" reason of which episcopacy is the scandalous, anti-Christian product.[3]

Because further reasoning about church government stands condemned as a sin against God's revealed will, Milton is free to articulate the historical and emotional stereotypes, largely derived from
Foxe's Booke of Martyrs,[4] which he knew would call forth a sympa-
thetic response from all antiprelatical English Protestants. The
historical myth is outlined in the first sentence, by the conventional
parallel between church history and the life of Christ:

> After the story of our Saviour Christ, suffering to the lowest
> bent of weaknesse, in the Flesh, and presently triumphing to the
> highest pitch of glory, in the Spirit, which drew up his body also,
> till we in both be united to him in the Revelation of his Kingdome:
> I do not know of any thing more worthy to take up the whole pas-
> sion of pitty, on the one side, and joy on the other: then to con-

27

sider first, the foule and sudden corruption, and then after many
a tedious age, the long-deferr'd, but much more wonderfull and
happy reformation of the Church in these latter dayes. [I:519]

As this introductory passage continues, the exclusively emotional
orientation of the tract becomes apparent. Long-winded hatred of
popery issues into its counterpart, sentimental panegyrics to the
Reformation:

> That such a Doctrine should through the grossenesse, and
> blindnesse, of her Professors, and the fraud of deceivable tra-
> ditions, drag so downwards, as to backslide one way into the
> Jewish beggery, of old cast rudiments, and stumble forward
> another way into the new-vomited Paganisme of sensuall Idola-
> try, attributing purity, or impurity, to things indifferent, that
> they might bring the inward acts of the Spirit to the outward,
> and customary ey-Service of the body, as if they could make
> God earthly, and fleshly, because they could not make them-
> selves heavenly and Spirituall. . . .
> When I recall to mind at last . . . how the bright and blissful
> Reformation (by Divine Power) strook through the black and
> settled Night of Ignorance and Antichristian Tyranny, me thinks
> a soveraigne and reviving joy must needs rush into the bosome
> of him that reads or heares; and the sweet Odour of the return-
> ing Gospell imbath his Soule with the fragrancy of Heaven.
> [I:520, 524]

Returning again and again to denunciations of the fleshly corruptions
wrought by popery and prelacy, Milton attempts to inflate these received Protestant attitudes and feelings into expressions of divine
wrath. Such a rhetorical objective, Milton seeking no less than to
make himself the voice of a nation of inspired prophets, rules out
more human and political modes of speech. Of Reformation is thus
the clearest and most deliberate example of Milton's tendency analyzed toward the end of the preceding chapter to perceive issues in
the context of his apocalyptic expectations.

This first of Milton's tracts has been called "a riot of graphic
diction."[5] Such native or "Elizabethan" diction is usually combined
with biblical echoes and more learned phrasings and cadences:

> But I trust they for whom God hath reserv'd the honour of Re-
> forming this Church will easily perceive their adversaries
> drift in thus calling for Antiquity, they feare the plain field of
> the Scriptures, the chase is too hot; they seek the dark, the
> bushie, the tangled Forrest, they would imbosk: they feel them-

selvs strook in the transparent streams of divine Truth, they
would plunge, and tumble, and thinke to ly hid in the foul weeds,
and muddy waters, where no plummet can reach the bottome.
But let them beat themselvs like Whales, and spend their oyl till
they be dradg'd ashoar: though wherfore should the Ministers
give them so much line for shifts, and delays? Wherfore should
they not urge only the Gospel, and hold it ever in their faces like
a mirror of Diamond, till it dazle, and pierce their misty ey
balls? maintaining it the honour of its absolute sufficiency and
supremacy inviolable: For if the Scripture be for Reformation,
and Antiquity to boot, 'tis but an advantage to the dozen, 'tis no
winning cast: and though Antiquity be against it, while the
Scriptures be for it, the Cause is as good as ought to be wisht,
Antiquity it selfe sitting Judge. [I:569–70]

The allusion to the Book of Revelation ("mirror of Diamond") is here
only part of the harmonious blend of elevated and homely language
that governs the passage. "But I trust they for whom God hath re-
serv'd the honour of Reforming this Church" modulates into "they
feare the plain field of the Scriptures" and then on down into the five
pithy monosyllables, "the chase is too hot." The lofty dignity suggested by the inverted and Latinate wording of "the honour of its
absolute sufficiency and supremacy inviolable" is followed by the
reference to throwing dice. These smooth transitions dignify the
common life of native Englishmen that is evoked by the "graphic"
diction, and, more to the rhetorical purpose, they suggest that the
simple Protestant emotions and mythology felt and believed by such
Englishmen are both heroic and prophetic.

This passage is also characteristic of Milton's use of imagery in
Of Reformation. Most of the details can be logically interpreted:
"where no plummet can reach the bottome" refers to the alleged fact
that the prelates' endless citations of the Fathers are part of an anti-
Christian conspiracy against intellectual clarity; "spend their oyl" is
a pun on the lamp oil the prelates depend on while they dredge up
their ancient, illegitimate authorities. But despite this local precision, the passage as a whole does not illustrate an exact correspondence between Milton's imagination and the real world. The shift
from a hunting to a fishing conceit, the rather incongruous appearance of a whale in the midst of the fishing conceit, and then the
further shift to dicing, all create a feeling of approximation. This
method is appropriate, in a way, to a tract which is not concerned
with arguing substantive proposals. As we shall see, the more
mimetic use of imagery and other imaginative devices in Areopagitica creates a coherent yet spacious context for practical reform.
Freedom to publish will help to constitute a society that flourishes

through the free play of all human creativity. Here, however, Milton
is concerned with the real world only insofar as the righteous English
Protestant recoils from it and in so doing judges it with the wrath of
God. To this purpose a continuous striving after inspired glimpses of
prelatical scandal is more appropriate than drawing coherent views of
it. Caring little for consistency, the rhetorical imagination allies itself in this tract not with reason but with a zeal that struggles toward
heavenly sublimity. With respect to its social implications, this kind
of imagination looks forward to the immediate and complete trans-
formation of society, not to its progressive reform. The daily life of
the fallen world, hunting, fishing, dicing is to escape from infection
and become something wholly new by means of the Gospel "mirror of
Diamond."

The syntax of the tract likewise seeks to foster the continuous expression of inspired outrage. Of Reformation provides more than
enough evidence to substantiate Hamilton's claim that the loose,
sprawling features of Milton's style can degenerate into mere ranting
when they are not organized by rational thought:[6]

> But it was Episcopacie that led the good and holy Men through the
> temptation of the Enemie, and the snare of this present world to
> many blame-worthy and opprobrious Actions. And it is still Epis-
> copacie that before all our eyes worsens and sluggs the most
> learned, and seeming religious of our Ministers, who no sooner
> advanc't to it, but like a seething pot set to coole, sensibly exhale
> and reake out the greatest part of that zeale, and those Gifts which
> were formerly in them, settling in a skinny congealment of ease
> and sloth at the top: and if they keep their Learning by some po-
> tent sway of Nature, 'tis a rare chance; but their devotion most
> commonly comes to that queazy temper of luke-warmnesse, that
> gives a Vomit to GOD himselfe. [I:536–37]

An element of hysteria is undeniably present in the passage. Milton
elaborates the same crude, sweeping accusations, running on until he
finds a particularly repulsive image with which to summarize them.
But the unloveliness of the passage is perhaps mitigated if we refer
to the argument in defense of scurrilous imagery which Milton makes
in the Apology. God himself is vehement and scurrilous when his
enemies deserve such violent denunciation. Only when he speaks with
the voice of God and God's Englishman is Milton justified in drawing
the shocking picture of divine vomit, the last decisive intensification
of the anger that runs throughout the passage. An ordinary polemic
might have ended with the word "Ministers," for to this point the passage assesses in a relatively sober and restrained manner, a socio-
logical phenomenon, the behavior patterns of upwardly-mobile clerics.

But the prophetic feelings the tract presumes to express can find
adequate release only in the sight of God, so Milton appends a trailing
relative pronoun clause ("Ministers, who . . ."), expanding on what is
meant by "worsens and sluggs" in the most vivid terms. Even this is
not sufficiently frenetic however; the ensuing coordinate clause which
appears to concede some lingering abilities in some prelates ("and if
they keep their Learning . . .") merely serves as a pretext for the
climactic ascent to indignant and scurrilous exaltation.

One additional example will suffice to represent the way in which
Milton consistently prolongs and extends his polemics until they become vehement enough to approximate a tone of saintly zeal. Concluding a discussion of Constantine's establishment of the church,
Milton begins with a simple, sober statement of the basic opposition:
"How should then the dim Taper of this Emperours age that had such
need of snuffing, extend any beame to our Times wherewith wee might
hope to be better lighted, then by those Luminaries that God hath set
up to shine to us far neerer hand" (I:556). He then describes Constantine's policy in greater detail:

> And what Reformation he wrought for his owne time it will not be
> amisse to consider, hee appointed certaine times for Fasts, and
> Feasts, built stately Churches, gave large Immunities to the
> Clergie, great Riches and Promotions to Bishops, gave and min-
> ister'd occasion to bring in a Deluge of Ceremonies, thereby
> either to draw in the Heathen by a resemblance of their rites, or
> to set a glosse upon the simplicity, and plainnesse of Christianity
> which to the gorgeous solemnities of Paganisme, and the sense of
> the Worlds Children seem'd but a homely and Yeomanly Religion,
> for the beauty of inward Sanctity was not within their prospect.
> [I:556]

In the subdued parallelisms ("he wrought . . . hee appointed . . . built
. . . gave . . . gave and minister'd . . ."), Milton seems to be doing
what he promises at the beginning, assembling the evidence and considering it in order to make a balanced and rational assessment of
Constantine's policies. But the structured analysis is thrown out of
balance when Milton appends a clause to the last member of the parallel series ("thereby either . . ."); this more detailed inquiry into
the institution of ceremonies soon begins to be conducted in the stock
formulas of Puritan hostility: "to set a glosse upon the simplicity,
and plainnesse of Christianity . . . ." The next clause is yet another
instance of the trailing effect ("Christianity which . . ."), as if the
litany of denunciation were to be further escalated, but in the last and
and loosest clause ("for the beauty of inward Sanctity was not within
their prospect"), denunciation is sacrificed to untroubled contempla-

tion. It is as if the first attempt to rise to an indignant climax had
been thwarted, as if God had led his prophetic propagandist through
all the usual syntactical devices only to bring him to rest in an isolated moment of calm and spiritual refreshment. Such moments are
rare in this tract, and Milton attacks anew in a manner that obliter-
ates this glimpse of true Christian principles:

> So that in this manner the Prelates both then and ever since
> comming from a meane, and Plebeyan Life on a sudden to be
> Lords of stately Palaces, rich furniture, delicious fare, and
> Princely attendance, thought the plaine and homespun verity of
> Christs Gospell unfit any longer to hold their Lordships ac-
> quaintance, unlesse the poore thred-bare Matron were put into
> better clothes; her chast and modest vaile surrounded with
> celestiall beames they overlai'd with wanton tresses, and in a
> flaring tire bespecckl'd her with all the gaudy allurements of a
> Whore. [I:556–57]

In this sentence the syntax is no more than a device for allowing the
epithets to pour out in a rhythm of steady intensification. The interpolated participial gives a reasonable explanation for the corruption
of the church ("comming from a meane, and Plebeyan Life . . ."), but
the main clause turns this shrewdness into sarcasm ("unfit any longer
. . . unlesse . . . better clothes"). The two additional amplifying
clauses ("her chast . . .") use this clothing imagery to transform sarcasm into righteous indignation, sweeping on into the wrathful trum-
pet tones of the Book of Revelation: "and in a flaring tire bespecckl'd
her with all the gaudy allurements of a Whore."
      The highly emotional texture is also sustained by containing all
the evils of prelacy within one or two very long sentences. The
speaker attempts to communicate them in one effusion in all the
passionate clarity with which they have been revealed to him. The
final denunciation before the apocalyptic prayer is such a passage.
Milton begins with a brief sketch of the nature of prelacy, "men that
beg so devoutly for the pride, and gluttony of their owne backs, and
bellies" (I:610), and then repeats these charges over and over in the
rest of the passage, adding new manifestations of the bishops' evil
practices each time around. The effect of straining towards a massive, coherent vision is created by the use of many forms of parallelism:

> Men that beg . . . that sue and sollicite so eagerly, . . . but for
> their Bishopricks, Deaneries, Prebends, and Chanonies; . . .
> They intreate us that we would not be weary of those insupport-
> able greevances that our shoulders have hitherto crackt under,
> they beseech us that we would think 'em fit to be our Justices of

of peace, our Lords, our highest officers of State, . . . they would
request us to indure still the russling of their Silken Cassocks,
. . . They pray us that it would please us to let them still hale us,
and worrey us with their band-dogs, and Pursivants; and that it
would please the Parliament that they may yet have the whipping,
fleecing, and fleaing of us in their diabolical Courts to tear the
flesh from our bones, and into our wide wounds instead of balm,
to power in the oil of Tartar, vitriol, and mercury. [I:610–12]

Since the parallelisms are concealed by the length and density of the
clauses separating the parallel elements, and since different types of
elements are used to make the parallels, the effect of driving emotional momentum is retained, but in this case the momentum is cir-
cular rather than linear. All levels of syntax erupt into patterns of
worldliness and tyranny. This final denunciation is both frenzied and
formal, a distillation of the prophetic outrage that runs all through
the tract.

The effort towards oracular, prophetic utterance is announced in
the first words of the tract, "Amidst those deepe and retired thoughts,"
and is developed by the sprawling syntax and immense, stereotyped
vision contained in the introductory pages.[7] This introduction sets the
ground rules for the rest of the pamphlet, defines the sense of un-
shakeable, inspired zeal that is manifested throughout in the ways I
have analyzed and is shown in its clearest form near the end in
Milton's impatient manner of dealing with objections: "At another
doubt of theirs I wonder; whether this discipline which we desire, be
such as can be put in practise within this Kingdom, they say it cannot
stand with the common Law, nor with the Kings safety; the government of Episcopacy is now so weav'd into the common Law: In Gods
name let it weave out againe; let not humain quillets keep back divine
authority" (I:605). Milton explicitly denies the importance of civil
prudence when set against his zealous apprehension that God is about
to transform England into Christ's kingdom on earth. This helps to
explain the unstructured quality of the tract. A writer whose goal is
to see in the prejudices of his audience the human expression of divine
wrath has no need for logical procedure or even for elegant rhetorical
planning. He need only convince his audience, by the devices of diction, imagery, and syntax I have analyzed, that their hostilities do indeed partake of the grandeur of God's wrath.
  Milton does claim to be following a logical procedure, first analyzing the past obstacles to complete reformation in England and then
the present ones (I:529, 542). But each stage of this argument turns
into historical narration, as Milton analyzes the past obstacles to
reformation by recounting the corruptions of sixteenth-century En-

gland. Those hindering reform in the present are "Antiquarians, Libertines, and Politicians." The libertines are dismissed in one paragraph. The antiquarians are answered by detailing the widespread corruption in the early church, the politicians by countless examples of papal intervention in European secular politics during the Middle Ages, and by the evidence of the universal misconduct of the prelates during the Stuart regimes. All periods of the established church are shown to have been anti-Christian. The structure of the tract is thus primarily designed to substantiate the stereotyped Foxean history grandiosely presented in the opening pages. As the voice of prophetic outrage suffuses this history of the universally fallen West, the tract becomes a preparation for the lurid apocalypse proclaimed in the final prayer (I:613-17).

But this prayer, both sentimental and cruelly vindictive, reveals the difficulties prophetic speech encounters when it is executed in Milton's manner. Northrop Frye explains the qualities of wrath in his description of Christ's haughty manner in Paradise Regained:

> The haughtiness and aloofness of Christ mean that, before Christ can work in the world, he must recognize and repudiate all worldliness. In Paradise Regained Christ is looking at the world as it is under the wrath, as the domain of Satan. Wrath is the reaction of goodness contemplating badness; it is disinterested and impersonal and is the opposite of anger or irritation.[8]

Milton and the other Puritans contemplating prelacy certainly do not in this tract achieve the disinterested impersonality of goodness contemplating badness. In view of the private reasons Milton had for engaging in pamphlet warfare, the significance of which I have noted in my introduction, it is not surprizing that a sense of personal anger and bitterness runs through this first tract and makes its prophetic rhetorical design difficult to credit. In the two other antiprelatical tracts I shall consider, Milton turns from this exclusive reliance on prophetic zeal and begins to assemble the rational and imaginative techniques of persuasion that are better suited to his objective of a reformed human society.

"The Reason of Church Government Urg'd against Prelaty"

Milton's fourth antiprelatical tract, The Reason of Church Government, was probably published in January or February 1642. Of the two works which intervene between it and Of Reformation, the first, Of Prelatical Episcopacy, is a specimen of "the blank opposing of biblical interpretations and the citation of a cloud of patristic witnesses"; the second, Animadversions, carries the highly emotional manner employed in Of Reformation to a new pitch of righteous

frenzy and contains another apocalyptic prayer. The new element in
The Reason of Church Government, the element that looks forward to
the later development of Milton's prose, is summed up in the title.
The tract attempts a coherent rational justification of the Presbyterian view of church government. Joan Webber has suggested that the
famous phrase, "the cool element of prose," in the personal digression refers to the calm, reasonable tone of the tract.[9] But the apparatus with which Milton encumbers everything but the personal
digression makes this an understatement. Each of the chapter titles
is a forbidding, Scholastic-like proposition, and the first few sentences of each chapter are usually a dry, logical justification of the
place of that chapter in the developing argument:

> We may returne now from this interposing difficulty thus remov'd,
> to affirme, that since Church-government is so strictly com-
> manded in Gods Word, the first and greatest reason why we should
> submit thereto, is because God hath so commanded. But whether
> of these two, Prelaty or Presbytery can prove it selfe to be sup-
> ported by this first and greatest reason, must be the next dispute.
> Wherein this position is to be first layd down as granted; that I
> may not follow a chase rather then an argument, that one of these
> two, and none other is of Gods ordaining, and if it be, that ordi-
> nance must be evident in the Gospell. [I:761–62]

But in practice the Presbyterian position still forbade any reasoning
other than the marshaling of biblical and patristic evidence. A kind
of reasoning of greater rhetorical interest is possible only by di-
gressing from the strict outline of the Presbyterian argument, and
this Milton does in the first chapter of the first book, the final chapter of the second book, and of course in the personal digression. At
these points, Milton "reasons" by releasing his social imagination,
and the tract suddenly changes from dry logical discourse into the
beginnings of a vision of social reform.[10] This development is antic-
ipated in the preface when Milton says that the question of church
government "containes in it the explication of many admirable and
heavenly privileges reacht out to us by the Gospell" (I:749).

Indeed this entire process of imaginative liberation is foreshad-
owed in the preface. The rhythm of the argument is slowed down by
devices of syntax and imagery.[11] Thus, the logic of the preface is
quite simple: Plato, a heathen, believed that eloquence and wisdom,
rather than fear, should be used to persuade men to obey civil laws.
Moses, certainly a better authority, taught the Jews true religion
and history so that they would choose to obey the Mosaic Law. In
view of these pre-Christian examples, free Christians obviously

should not blindly follow tradition, but should learn the structure of
their liberty, the true "reason of church government." And Milton
therefore, amidst the babble of prelates, has written a discourse expounding the true principles of Christian liberty and discipline, which
are embodied in Presbyterian church government. But the rhetorical
amplification of this argument begins with the very first sentence:
"In the publishing of humane lawes, which for the most part aime not
beyond the good of civill society, to set them barely forth to the people without reason or Preface, like a physicall prescript, or only with
threatnings, as it were a lordly command, in the judgement of Plato
was thought to be done neither generously nor wisely" (I:746). This
sentence is supremely formal and Ciceronian, consisting as it does
of a series of suspensions ("In the publishing . . . to set them barely
forth . . . in the judgement . . .") followed by a main clause which
ends the sentence with two emphatic adverbs ("neither generously
nor wisely").[12] In addition to creating an effect of spacious elevation
and formal completion, the sentence is relaxed enough to allow interpolation of a precise definition ("humane lawes, which for the most
part aime not beyond the good of civill society") and of copious elaboration ("without reason or Preface, like a physicall prescript, or
only with threatnings, as it were a lordly command"). Milton pauses
to appreciate Plato's wise judgement as he begins his discussion,
hinting that the issue at hand involves far more than fine points of
scriptural exegesis. This impression is strengthened by the next
sentence, which begins to insinuate that an entire reformed nation
could live spaciously, by freely choosing to govern itself by truth:

> His advice was, seeing that persuasion certainly is a more win-
> ning, and more manlike way to keepe men in obedience then feare,
> that to such lawes as were of principall moment, there should be
> us'd as an induction, some well temper'd discourse, shewing how
> good, how gainfull, how happy it must needs be to live according
> to honesty and justice, which being utter'd with those native col-
> ours and graces of speech, as true eloquence the daughter of
> vertue can best bestow upon her mothers praises, would so incite,
> and in a manner, charme the multitude into the love of that which
> is really good as to imbrace it ever after, not of custome and
> awe, which most men do, but of choice and purpose, with true and
> constant delight. [I:746]

It is as if the elevated Ciceronian mode of the first sentence, brought
to a beautiful climax with the words "generously" and "wisely," had
put into Milton's mind a sketch of a truly generous and free society.
Filling out the explicit logic, it seems, is the logic of social vision,
in which each thought seems to call forth its own imaginative elabo-

ration. This more associative logic demands a looser syntax, yet if
it is to form itself into a coherent vision, it must retain some of the
Ciceronian firmness and dignity. The first half of this sentence,
therefore, continues the Ciceronian style of the first sentence. The
main clause is introduced, delayed by necessary interpolations and
an inversion ("seeing that . . . to such lawes . . . as an induction
. . ."), and completed by firmly naming the central concept of the
preface ("some well temper'd discourse . . ."). From this point the
idea of a persuasive "well temper'd discourse" is turned into a
source of national heroism in two dependent clauses, one ("shewing
. . .") closely tied to the primary syntax, the other ("which . . .") a
trailing clause removed from its antecedent. The trailing clause
contains its own interpolations ("being utter'd . . . and in a manner,
charm . . ."), an interpolation within one of these interpolations ("as
true eloquence . . ."), and its own dependent amplifying clause ("not
of custome . . . but of choice . . ."), which in turn includes an interpolated phrase ("which most men do . . .") and a further amplification ("with true and constant delight"). The suspended first half of
the sentence seems to store up energy which is released into the
second half by the crucial words, "well temper'd discourse." Throughout the looser second half, doubling and tripling of nouns and adjectives having to do with virtue and happiness create a sense of copious
fullness of vision. Because these words are scattered across the
sentence, there is also a sense of leisurely expansiveness, which is
increased by the interpolated personifications of eloquence and virtue.
The key grammatical elements of the long trailing clause are also
widely scattered ("which . . . would so incite . . . the multitude . . . as
to imbrace it . . ."), so that the conclusion of the subsidiary amplifying
clause seems to draw all the elements together into the furthest and
deepest extension of the vision, a compact and balanced view of fulfilled
active virtue: "but of choice and purpose, with true and constant delight."

    In the remainder of the preface, Milton continues to expatiate with-
in and beyond the limits of his logical outline. Beginning the next
stage of the argument ("a better & more ancient authority . . ."), he is
drawn into contemplation of the Bible: "and indeed being a point of so
high wisdome & worth, how could it be but we should find it in that
book, within whose sacred context all wisdom is infolded?" (I:747).
At the logical turn, when he says that Christians above all others
should be informed by reason, he presses forward with an emphatic
appositive clause which gives a more precise description of disciplined freedom: "especially for that the church hath in her immediate
cure those inner parts and affections of the mind where the seat of
reason is; having power to examine our spirituall knowledge, and to

demand from us in Gods behalfe a service intirely reasonable" (I:
747–48). And after the logical argument is completed by Milton's
statement of the purpose of his tract, he deals with the possible objection that he is too young for such a wise eloquence and goes on to
state his more generous purposes in the passage already partially
quoted: "and for the task . . . Christ Jesus" (I:749–50).[13]

In the first chapter of the first book, the logic is again fairly
straightforward: church government, or discipline, is the sine qua
non of all human accomplishment. It is the outward form of virtue
on earth and determines the shape of New Jerusalem. The church,
therefore, must like everything else be bound together by discipline.
But even in secular affairs discipline can be framed only by divinely
inspired men of heroic virtue, as is demonstrated by the fact that
ordinary men are incapable even of disciplining their own households. The ordering of the church, "the elect household of God,"
must therefore be the work of the church's father and husband; that
is to say, it must be set forth in the Bible. Again the syntax functions as a source of contemplative refreshment, restraining the
momentum of this argument. And as in the preface, this contemplation seems most liberating during the logically subordinate descrip-
tions of secular affairs. Although their syntax is simple and direct,
Milton creates an effect of firmness and coherence in the first three
important sentences of the chapter by again building to an emphatic
climax:

> For there is not that thing in the world of more grave and urgent
> importance throughout the whole life of man, then is discipline
> . . . . He that hath read with judgement, of Nations and Common-
> wealths, of Cities and Camps of peace and warre, sea and land,
> will readily agree that the flourishing and decaying of all civill
> societies, all the moments and turnings of humane occasions are
> mov'd to and fro as upon the axle of discipline. So that whatso-
> ever power or sway in mortall things weaker men have attributed
> to fortune, I durst with more confidence (the honour of divine
> providence ever sav'd) ascribe either to the vigor, or the slack-
> nesse of discipline. [I:751]

The word "discipline" provides the syntactical discipline for this
passage, functioning as decisive punctuation. Each sentence comes
to rest on the subject of the entire discussion. But the mere word in
the first sentence expands into more resonant phrases in the other
two sentences ("axle of discipline . . . the vigor, or the slacknesse of
discipline"), and this is part of a general loosening and amplifying
process, a process which does not weaken the coherence of Milton's
presentation. Thus the second sentence is a copious restatement of

the first, which is to say it is an imaginative extension and enrichment of the concept of discipline. The third more loosely framed
sentence ("So that . . .") extends the concept further by associating
it with the relation between providence and free will. Of the next
two general statements, the first is a straightforward coordinate
sentence, the second a complex mixture of a simple sentence joined
to a suspended one which branches out into a loose amplifying clause:

> Nor is there any sociable perfection in this life civill or sacred
> that can be above discipline, but she is that which with her musi-
> call cords preserves and holds all the parts thereof together . . . .
> And certainly discipline is not only the removall of disorder, but
> if any visible shape can be given to divine things, the very visible
> shape and image of vertue, whereby she is not only seene in the
> regular gestures and motions of her heavenly paces as she walkes,
> but also makes the harmony of her voice audible to mortall eares.
> [I:751–52]

Here the process of imaginative growth and enrichment continues. In
the first sentence "discipline" is removed to the end of the first
clause; in the second it is surrounded by less important words in the
middle of the first clause. The key word has been replaced in the
syntactically prominent positions by the progressively richer and
livelier definitions of the concept it names. These definitions are
articulated by the traditional imagery which begins with "axle of discipline," becomes a personification in "she is that which with her
musicall cords preserves and holds all the parts thereof together,"
and grows into a living being in "the very visible shape and image of
vertue, whereby she is not only seene in the regular gestures and
motions of her heavenly paces as she walkes, but also makes the
harmony of her voice audible to mortall eares." It is important to
note that the process of syntactical relaxation stands in direct relation to this coherent, imaginative growth of the concept of discipline.
The loosest construction so far ("whereby . . ."), which flows smoothly from a firmly stated abstract redefinition ("the very visible shape
and image of vertue, . . ."), is the vehicle Milton chooses for the
graceful portrait just quoted. The freedom of Milton's syntax becomes
quite precisely the disciplined freedom of his moral imagination.
 Further extending what is by now a vision of discipline into heaven,
Milton soon elaborates the copious syntax to the point of extravagance:

> Yet it is not to be conceiv'd that those eternall effluences of sanc-
> tity and love in the glorified Saints should by this meanes be con-
> fin'd and cloy'd with repetition of that which is prescrib'd, but that
> our happinesse may orbe it selfe into a thousand vagancies of glory
> and delight, and with a kind of eccentricall equation be as it were

> an invariable Planet of joy and felicity, how much lesse can we
> believe that God would leave his fraile and feeble, though not
> lesse beloved Church here below to the perpetuall stumble of
> conjecture and disturbance in this our darke voyage without the
> card and compasse of Discipline. [I:752–53]

The doubling in this sentence is so copious it almost succeeds in
creating onomatopoeia in prose. That is to say, one doublet may
create a sense of balance and harmony. Repeated doubling will combine this effect with a feeling of superabundant vitality, and this fusion is just what Milton is talking about.[14] Furthermore, although
the doublets in the second clause are certainly gloomy, they unavoidably partake of the energetic regularity of the first clause, especially
since they are completed by the emphatically positive phrase, "the
card and compasse of Discipline." The second clause is tied to the
first in other ways. The astronomical imagery of the first clause is
certainly related to the navigational imagery of the second. One may
even see the travelers on the "darke voyage" looking up at the invariable planets of joy and felicity towards which the card and com-
pass of discipline is leading them. This generous imagery develops
as the syntax continues to loosen and amplify the discussion. It is
introduced in the second half of the antithesis within the first clause
("Yet it is not to be conceiv'd . . . but that our happinesse may orbe
it selfe into a thousand vagancies of glory and delight"), and in an
additional coordinate phrase it offers a more precise view of heavenly discipline ("and with a kind of eccentricall equation be as it
were an invariable Planet of joy and felicity"). Again syntactical
freedom is the occasion for imaginative gain. Finally, a confused
grammatical turn makes the two main components of the sentence
seem part of one vision. Logically, the sentence should read, "seeing
that it is not to be conceiv'd . . . how much lesse can we believe . . . ."
Whether intended or not, the absence of such grammatical subordination blurs the contrast between earth and heaven and creates the impression that the second clause is associatively related to the first:
joyful heavenly discipline and church discipline are both parts of one
universal order. This impression is confirmed by the next sentence:

> Which is so hard to be of mans making, that we may see even in
> the guidance of a civill state to worldly happinesse, it is not for
> every learned, or every wise man, though many of them consult
> in common, to invent or frame a discipline, but if it be at all the
> worke of man, it must be of such a one as is a true knower of
> himselfe, and himselfe in whom contemplation and practice, wit,
> prudence, fortitude, and eloquence must be rarely met, both to
> comprehend the hidden causes of things, and span in his thoughts

all the various effects that passion or complexion can worke in
mans nature; and hereto must his hand be at defiance with gaine,
and his heart in all vertues heroick. [I:753]

This entire sentence is, strictly speaking, another trailing clause
loosely related to the previous sentence, stemming from "Discipline,"
the final word of that sentence. Thus, in the course of proving that a
pattern of church government must be found in the Bible, Milton, by
including heaven, the church, and secular life in one long, loose sentence, creates a broad vision of universal discipline and freedom, one
that could open the way for all sorts of reforms besides the one being
considered in this tract.

The last chapter of the second book seems to stand in a balanced
relation to the first chapter of the first book. The latter offers a
prospect of the importance of discipline on all levels of the universe;
the former gives a detailed account of the operation of true discipline
in the individual soul. In this last chapter Milton moves explicitly
beyond his logical outline. Having proved that secular coercion by
prelatical courts contradicts the Gospel, which is all that is promised
in the chapter title, he goes on with this long narration of the process
of true spiritual discipline, which is also a view of the ideal Christian
community. The loose, exfoliating sentence structure which is Milton's stock in trade here again functions to obscure the logical transitions in the argument and thus to clarify the free flowing relationship
between the wayward individual sinner and the other members of the
church who judge him;

And look by how much the internal man is more excellent and
noble then the external, by so much is his cure more exactly,
more throughly, and more particularly to be perform'd. For
which cause the holy Ghost by the Apostles joyn'd to the minister,
as assistant in this great office sometimes a certain number of
grave and faithful brethren, (for neither doth the phisitian doe all
in restoring his patient, he prescribes, another prepares the
med'cin, some tend, some watch, some visit) much more may a
minister partly not see all, partly erre as a man: besides that
nothing can be more for the mutuall honour and love of the people to their Pastor, and his to them, then when in select numbers
and courses they are seen partaking, and doing reverence to the
holy duties of discipline by their serviceable, and solemn presence, and receiving honour again from their imployment, not now
any more to be separated in the Church by vails and partitions as
laicks and unclean, but admitted to wait upon the tabernacle as
the rightfull Clergy of Christ, a chosen generation, a royal Priest-

hood to offer up spiritual sacrifice in that meet place to which
God and the Congregation shall call and assigne them. [I:837–38]

Barker (pp. 34–36) sees in this insistence on the dignity of laymen a
sign of Milton's incipient radicalism that was soon to reveal itself
more fully in the divorce tracts. The passage is also like the first
chapter of the first book because it anticipates the rhetorical method
of the divorce tracts and Areopagitica. The turn from the individual
to the community is handled with fairly exact logic. Since the disciplining of the inner man is of such urgent significance, the minister
obviously needs assistance in carrying it out, a point well understood
by the Holy Ghost. The medical analogy is of course intended to reinforce this logic. In the rest of the sentence, Milton transcends
mere logic and celebrates the only genuine church community, one
that would embrace both clergymen and laymen. Again, it is the relatively loose syntax that makes this possible. The first of the two
appended clauses shifts the focus of the argument outward, from the
individual reprobate to the compassionate community, but does so
with a rather casual conjunction, suggesting the continuity both of the
discourse and of the communal life of the faithful: "besides that
nothing can be more for the mutuall honour and love of the people to
their Pastor, and his to them." If we discipline the souls of men the
only way they can be disciplined, we immediately discover "besides"
that this one reform has beneficial consequences for the style of our
living together in general. The second appended clause proceeds to
celebrate this regenerated community, confronting the impositions
of prelates and transcending them with exuberant paeans to the dignity and priesthood of all believers: "not now any more to be separated in the Church by vails and partitions as laicks and unclean, but
admitted . . . as the rightfull Clergy of Christ, a chosen generation,
a royal Priesthood."

The same pattern recurs when the final point of the argument for
admitting laymen to participate in such important church functions
as discipline, a man's desire to enjoy the good opinion and good
fellowship of his brethren, is used to ease the center of the discussion back towards the individual sinner. This consideration of
shame naturally leads into a hymn to a nobler inner incentive to
virtue and piety, self-reverence, and, argues Milton, one way to instill self-reverence in the individual laymen is to allow him to participate in the offices of church discipline. What we see, then, is
that Barker's point about incipient radicalism and mine about imaginative momentum are related: Milton's prose style not only encour-
ages but virtually thrusts his thought towards broader and more
comprehensive vision, and this in turn generates his rather eccentric
form of social and political radicalism.

In both chapters, these expressions of a rational and imaginative idealism occur in a social vacuum. They are essentially digressions from the main task of the tract: "Reason . . . Urg'd against Prelaty." Perhaps this provides one explanation of the relation of the personal digression to the rest of the tract. An explicit digression can completely ignore the polemical burdens imposed on the idealist by a deformed social reality and can thus give unstinted expression to the pleasures of imaginative reasoning. In any case, the digression considered by itself forms an imaginative progression similar to those in the two chapters already analyzed. A discussion of the reasons that led Milton to engage in pamphleteering develops into a hymn to his poetic aspirations. The following sentence culminates this process:

These abilities, wheresoever they be found, are the inspired guift of God rarely bestow'd, but yet to some (though most abuse) in every Nation: and are of power beside the office of a pulpit, to imbreed and cherish in a great people the seeds of vertu, and publick civility, to allay the pertubations of the mind, and set the affections in right tune, to celebrate in glorious and lofty Hymns the throne and equipage of Gods Almightinesse, and what he works, and what he suffers to be wrought with high providence in his Church, to sing the victorious agonies of Martyrs and Saints, the deeds and triumphs of just and pious Nations doing valiantly through faith against the enemies of Christ, to deplore the general relapses of Kingdoms and States from justice and Gods true worship. Lastly, whatsoever in religion is holy and sublime, in vertu amiable, or grave, whatsoever hath passion or admiration in all the changes of that which is call'd fortune from without, or the wily suttleties and refluxes of mans thoughts from within, all these things with a solid and treatable smoothnesse to paint out and describe. Teaching over the whole book of sanctity and vertu through all the instances of example with such delight to those especially of soft and delicious temper who will not so much as look upon Truth herselfe, unlesse they see her elegantly drest, that whereas the paths of honesty and good life appear now rugged and difficult, though they be indeed easy and pleasant, they would then appear to all men both easy and pleasant though they were rugged and difficult indeed. [I:816–18]

As we have seen several times previously in this discussion of the antiprelatical tracts, a passage which will ascend to an oh altitudo begins rather quietly, minimizing the significance and potency of the imagination in human affairs: "These abilities . . . rarely bestow'd . . . (though most abuse) . . . are of power beside the office of a pulpit." From this point, however, the passage takes off into a realm in which the imagination flows out unimpeded into a regenerated society, easily embracing and articulating all significant themes. The structure of this major part of the passage is based on a parallel series of infinitives: "to imbreed and cherish . . . to allay . . . and set . . . to celebrate . . . to sing . . . to deplore . . . to paint out and describe." The most exciting characteristic of the passage, however, is the rhythmic variation of each of these infinitive units. Each one seems to find its own proper shape, producing a sense of vitality within the ordered parallel structure. The first two are firmly balanced: "to imbreed and cherish . . . the seeds of vertu, and publick civility, to allay the perturbations . . . and set the affections." The next two swell out with greater amplitude, each constituted by subsidiary flexible parallelisms: "to celebrate . . . the throne and equipage . . . and what he works, and what he suffers to be wrought . . . to sing the victorious agonies . . . the deeds and triumphs." The next member is the simplest of the series and is a prelude to the exuberant final member: "to deplore the general relapses . . . ." Finally, the last member produces a definite sense of climax, by inverting the order and placing the infinitive at the end and by alluding to Saint Paul's syntax with an energetically varied subsidiary parallel series:[15] "Lastly, whatsoever in religion . . . in vertu . . . whatsoever hath passion or admiration . . . fortune from without, . . . mans thoughts from within." This sense of climax is confirmed when Milton transcends the formal structure with an absolute participial clause ("Teaching over . . . difficult indeed") which has a quite definite meaning: the themes of a lofty imagination simply flow on irresistibly into a perfectly reformed, "imaginative" social order, in which the consequences of the Fall are precisely reversed: "that whereas the paths of honesty and good life appear now rugged and difficult, though they be indeed easy and pleasant, they would then appear to all men easy and pleasant though they were rugged and difficult indeed."[16]

One of the Yale editors claims that structurally the tract combines the Puritan sermon and the classical oration.[17] The digression and the two most interesting chapters, at least, do attempt to enrich Puritanism with Renaissance humanism. The first chapter is explicable only in this way, because from a strict Presbyterian view, it contains superfluous human reasoning. Save for this humanist orientation, there is no need to expose the unsoundness of church discipline that has been humanly devised; one need only point out the relevant passages of Scripture, as Milton does in the next chapter. The account of practical discipline in the last chapter is likewise a humanistic extension of scriptural command:

I dare assure my self that every true protestant will admire the
integrity, the uprightnes, the divine and gracious purposes therof,
and even for the reason of it so coherent with the doctrine of the
Gospel, besides the evidence of command in Scripture, will con-
fesse it to be the only true Church-government. [I:834–35]

The personal digression, however, envisioning an alliance between
piety, public virtue, and poetry, relatively free of the excesses of
Puritan zeal, is a far more coherent fusion of human creativity and
Protestant reform. In Areopagitica this "undigested lump" of perfected idealism is energized, as it were, into a socially creative im-
pulse that infiltrates and invigorates an entire tract.

As stated above, however, most of the tract is polemic. Sometimes
the attack is conducted urbanely, as when Milton shapes an image into
a neat polemical thrust:

I say Prelaty thus ascending in a continuall pyramid upon pretence
to perfect the Churches unity, if notwithstanding it be found most
needfull, yea the utmost helpe to dearn up the rents of schisme by
calling a councell, what does it but teach us that Prelaty is of no
force to effect this work which she boasts to be her maister-peice;
and that her pyramid aspires and sharpens to ambition, not to
perfection, or unity. [I:790]

Another tactic is to speed up the pace of argument, making one kind
of clever rebuttal after another so that the Anglican position begins
to seem pitifully inadequate, a kind of airy nothing through which
Milton's deft logic effortlessly races:

Why should the performance of ordination which is a lower office
exalt a Prelat, and not the seldome discharge of a higher and
more noble office which is preaching & administring much rather
depresse him? Verily neither the nature, nor the example of ordination doth any way require an imparity betweene the ordainer
and the ordained. For what more naturall then every like to produce his like, man to beget man, fire to propagate fire, and in
examples of highest opinion the ordainer is inferior to the ordained; for the Pope is not made by the precedent Pope, but by
Cardinals, who ordain and consecrate to a higher and greater
office then their own. [I:768]

But the bishops are knaves as well as fools, and so Milton frequently
indulges in the kind of simple, raging denunciation that controls the
tone in Of Reformation. Whether witty or shrill, however, Milton's
attacks have little rhetorical connection with the positive visions
which open up most generously at the beginning, middle, and end.
When they are not separated into different chapters, these two modes

of discourse sit uneasily together in the same chapter. For example,
two of the eloquent sentences in the first chapter simply trail off at
the end into topical references, in a manner corresponding precisely
to the structure of the sentence from the Apology discussed in the
preceding chapter:

> And his heart in all vertues heroick. So far is it from the kenne
> of these wretched projectors of ours that bescraull their Pamflets
> every day with new formes of government for our Church . . .
> more pliant to the soule, and usefull to the Common-wealth:
> which if men were but as good to discipline themselves, as some
> are to tutor their Horses and Hawks, it could not be so grosse in
> most housholds. [I:753–54]

In the last chapter, Milton continually interrupts his vision of a regenerated church community with tirades against the present haughty
exclusion of laymen from full participation. To be sure, the isolated
utilizations of polemical wit in this pamphlet do begin to transform
prelacy from a demonic monstrosity into a rhetorically and humanly
manageable opponent. God's apocalyptic wrath is no longer the only
Presbyterian weapon, but the gap between high ideals and fallen reality remains very wide.

In The Reason of Church Government, then, the persuasive method
that will characterize the divorce tracts and Areopagitica makes its
first appearance, but since the real social world is apparently still
dominated by the prelatical monster, this method can only express
itself in personal idealism, it cannot shape itself into a social vision.
There remains a discontinuity between "beholding the bright counte-
nance of truth" in "a calme and pleasing solitarynes," and "imbarking
in a troubl'd sea of noises and hoars disputes." Milton's rhetoric will
begin to accommodate the real world, as well as discharge itself
against it, only when Milton can believe or pretend to believe that
England has truly begun to repair the ruins of our first parents. This
will mean that social reality will have started to do what Milton requires of it, meet his exacting standards more than halfway. At such
a point, Milton can relax the tone of his writing, deal with his political
and polemical opponents somewhat less zealously, somewhat more
satirically. We have seen the beginnings of this tempering of rhetorical emotion in this tract, in the fragmentary urbanity of the polemic.
We shall see it carried much further in the Apology.

"An Apology against a Pamphlet"

Milton's Animadversions provoked somebody, probably Bishop Hall
and/or his son, into publishing A Modest Confutation of the Animadversions. Milton hastened into print sometime in April 1642 with a

reply burdened with a title page which encompasses the entire dreary
controversy: An Apology against a Pamphlet Call'd A Modest Confutation of the Animadversions upon the Remonstrant against Smectym-
nuus. William R. Parker says of this last antiprelatical tract that
"more than any of its predecessors the Apology is a pamphlet of
great stylistic variety, as though its author was deliberately exhib-
iting the many facets of his skill."[18] Certainly more often than in
any of the previous tracts Milton here tells the reader about his
stylistic modulations:

> There while they acted, and overacted, among other young schol-
> ars, I was a spectator; they thought themselves gallant men, and
> I thought them fools, they made sport, and I laught, they mis-
> pronounc't and I mislik't, and to make up the atticisme, they were
> out, and I hist . . . that I may after this harsh discord touch upon
> a smoother string, awhile to entertaine my selfe and him that list,
> with some more pleasing fit. [I:887, 922]

No doubt these insinuations of literary agility are intended "to pluck
out of the heads of [the] admirers [of prelacy] the conceit that all who
are not Prelaticall, are grosse-headed, thick witted, illiterat, shallow" (I:873). But these comments are only the incidental part of the
literary and rhetorical analysis found throughout the tract. Vehe-
mence is defended by scriptural precept and by the classical principle
that persuasive techniques should fit the audience and the occasion.
Satire, born of tragedy, is by definition sharp and vigorous, not
"toothless." Quality of style depends on the quality of an author's
relation to moral truth. In short, Milton is in this work more consciously concerned with the rhetorical effectiveness of Protestant
values and passions, a concern he summarizes in the following tab-
leau vivant:

> Some also were indu'd with a staid moderation, and soundnesse of
> argument to teach and convince the rationall and sober-minded;
> yet not therefore that to be thought the only expedient course of
> teaching, for in times of opposition when either against new
> heresies arising, or old corruptions to be reform'd this coole un-
> passionate mildnesse of positive wisdome is not anough to damp
> and astonish the proud resistance of carnall, and false Doctors,
> then (that I may have leave to soare a while as the Poets use) then
> Zeale whose substance is ethereal, arming in compleat diamond
> ascends his fiery Chariot drawn with two blazing Meteors figur'd
> like beasts, but of a higher breed then any the Zodiack yeilds,
> resembling two of those four which Ezechiel and S. John saw, the
> one visag'd like a Lion to expresse power, high autority and in-
> dignation, the other of count'nance like a man to cast derision and

> scorne upon perverse and fraudulent seducers: with these the
> invincible warriour Zeale shaking loosely the slack reins drives
> over the heads of Scarlet Prelats, and such as are insolent to
> maintaine traditions, brusing their stiffe necks under his flaming
> wheels. [I:900]

Thus Milton retrospectively justifies the style of his first, third, and
part of his fourth tracts; given the nature of his opponents, a zealous,
extrarational style was a rhetorical imperative. But this gorgeous
imaginative summary of that former style is itself similar to the
more coherent enthusiasms of the most interesting sections of The
Reason of Church Government. As in those sections of the earlier
work, the passage turns from reasoning about rhetorical necessity
to imaginative appreciation of rhetorical possibility, and again this
movement occurs in an idealistic vacuum. What is new here is the
self-consciousness of the passage, the suggestion of a deliberate ex-
periment in elevated prose rhetoric. The tract contains several other
exercises in soaring "a while," most of them explicitly identified as
such: the introductory section, the autobiographical digression, and
the political digression praising Parliament to the skies. Similarly,
the format of point by point rebuttal of the Modest Confuter is ex-
ploited to temper zealous hatred of episcopacy with urbane and liter-
ate satire. I am tempted to speculate that in the Apology Milton began
trying to write prose with his right hand, began trying to perceive it
as a medium which might give full and free expression to his poetic
ideals, and began developing a voice of sufficient range and flexibility
to perform this task.

   Since the celebration of Parliament is the most explicit of the many
essays at gorgeous high eloquence, one specimen from this section
will suffice to show the kind of thing Milton is doing elsewhere as well:

> Nor did they deceave that expectation which with the eyes and de-
> sires of their countrey was fixt upon them; for no sooner did the
> force of so much united excellence meet in one globe of bright-
> nesse and efficacy, but encountring the dazl'd resistance of tyranny,
> they gave not over, though their enemies were strong and suttle,
> till they had laid her groveling upon the fatall block. With one
> stroke winning againe our lost liberties and Charters, which our
> forefathers after so many battels could scarce maintaine. And
> meeting next, as I may so resemble, with the second life of tyranny
> (for she was growne an ambiguous monster, and to be slaine in two
> shapes) guarded with superstition which hath no small power to
> captivate the minds of men otherwise most wise, they neither were
> taken with her miter'd hypocrisie, nor terrifi'd with the push of her

bestiall hornes, but breaking them immediately forc't her to un-
bend the pontificall brow, and recoil. Which repulse only, given
to the Prelats (that we may imagine how happy their removall
would be) was the producement of such glorious effects and consequences in the Church, that if I should compare them with those
exployts of highest fame in Poems and <u>Panegyricks</u> of old, I am
certaine it would but diminish and impaire their worth, who are
now my argument. [I:924–25]

The fact that the sentences here are not so open-ended as in previous tracts emphasizes that the passage is a tour de force. Milton is
modeling himself on classical orators, so he writes more strictly
Ciceronian prose. In each sentence Parliament meets its enemies
in open combat in a series of subordinate clauses, then crushes them
in a resolving main clause. And in each case an amplifying coda
rounds off the sentence by indicating the far-reaching consequences
of these heroic gestures: "With one stroke winning againe our lost
liberties . . . Which repulse only . . . was the producement of such
glorious effects and consequences in the Church." We are relaxing
here far above the battle in a realm of perfected idealism. Or rather,
this realm has come into existence because Milton pretends the battle
has been won. As the Yale editors note, the first of the sentences
quoted refers to the execution of Strafford, the second to the exclusion
of bishops from the House of Lords and perhaps also to the impeach-
ment of Archbishop Laud (I:924–25, nn. 40–42). Milton does not adapt
his rhetoric to the real world, even provisionally. He never does that.
Instead, he makes the real world adapt itself to his rhetoric and to his
explicitly literary universe. He absorbs these two or three events
into a patterned eloquence, seeking to embody that still time beyond
chiding which is his goal for all political reform.

The satirical polemic occupies most of the tract. Milton's tech-
nique, like that of the footnotes to <u>The Dunciad</u>, is to scrutinize the
Confuter's unguarded assertions and subject them to Milton's own
extravagent elaborations. The result is to place the Confuter at the
center of another literary universe, a grotesque world which is the
precise antithesis of the realm articulated in the high style of the
idealistic set pieces. The diction of these passages is vigorously
earthy, and the syntax moves at a nervous, rapid pace, each clever
characterization of the Confuter leading smoothly into another even
more telling one:

And because he pretends to be a great conjector at other men by
their writings, I will not faile to give ye, Readers, a present taste
of him from his own title; hung out like a toling signe-post to call
passengers, not simply a <u>confutation</u> but <u>a modest confutation</u> with

a laudatory of it selfe obtruded in the very first word. Whereas
a modest title should only informe the buyer what the book containes without furder insinuation, this officious epithet so hastily
assuming the modesty wch others are to judge of by reading, not
the author to anticipate to himselfe by forestalling, is a strong
presumption that his modesty set there to sale in the frontispice,
is not much addicted to blush. A surer signe of his lost shame
he could not have given, then seeking thus unseasonably to pre-
possesse men of his modesty. And seeing he hath neither kept
his word in the sequel, nor omitted any kind of boldnesse in
slandering, tis manifest his purpose was only to rub the forehead
of his title with this word modest, that he might not want colour
to be the more impudent throughout his whole confutation. [I:875–
76]

The impression of rapid movement is largely a consequence of the
density of polemical wit in the passage. A more important effect is
that of pattern and coherence, produced by both syntax and diction.
The imagery of commerce and cosmetics and words suggesting grace-
lessness ("obtruded . . . so hastily assuming . . . unseasonably . . .
boldnesse . . . impudent . . .") combine to portray a being behaving in
accordance with the laws of its own strangely perverse nature. The
syntax develops this impression in two ways: by subordinate clauses
governed by logical connectives, in the first and last sentences quoted,
and by antithetical contrast, in the second sentence. In the first sentence, the "toling signe-post" image and the unseemly "obtruded"
seem to follow logically from "And because. . . ." The logical connection
is less tenuous in the last sentence ("And seeing . . . tis manifest . . .").
In addition, the harmonious cadences of the two clauses of this last sentence reinforce the impression that the Confuter behaves according to
his own devious and contorted logic: "He hath neither kept his word
in the sequel, nor omitted any kind of boldnesse in slandering . . . his
purpose was only to rub the forehead of his title with this word modest, that he might not want colour to be the more impudent throughout
his whole confutation."[19] In the second sentence ("Whereas . . .
blush.") the contrast between true and false modesty is made perfectly clear before the pungent conclusion by a major and a minor
antithesis, so that the conclusion itself seems a satisfying fulfillment
of a pattern of opposition.

But all this is only the beginning of a larger satirical pattern, for
as Milton continues to examine the few words on the Confuter's title
page, he uncovers an apparently endless network of grotesque behavior, reaching back through all the title pages on the Anglican side of
the Smectymnuuan controversy to Bishop Hall's earlier effeminate
sermons and tracts (I:876–77). A few pages later, again showing up
the Confuter's absurd bungling ("But in an ill houre hath his unfortu-

nate rashnesse stumbl'd upon the mention of miming," I:880), Milton
explores the satirical possibilities with real exuberance, seeing in
Bishop Hall's "toothless" satire, Mundus Alter & Idem, a perfect
specimen of the bizarre harmonies of the prelatical world view.

> The maker, or rather the anticreator of that universall foolery,
> who he was, who like that other principle of the Maniches the
> Arch evill one, when he had look't upon all that he had made and
> mapt out, could say no other but contrary to the Divine Mouth,
> that it was all very foolish . . . . this petty prevaricator of
> America, the zanie of Columbus, (for so he must be till his
> worlds end) having rambl'd over the huge topography of his own
> vain thoughts, no marvell, if he brought us home nothing but a
> meer tankard drollery, a venereous parjetory for a stewes.
> [I:880–81]

In contrast to The Reason of Church Government, this satirical
dimension creates a context out of which the passages of virtuoso
eloquence can plausibly arise. Milton comments on the desirability
of plausible transitions after the formal eulogy of Parliament:

> And how to break off suddenly into those jarring notes, which this
> Confuter hath set me, I must be wary, unlesse I can provide against
> offending the eare, as some Musicians are wont skilfully to fall out
> of one key into another without breach of harmony. [I:928][20]

In this tract Milton does for the most part "provide against offending
the eare." The fluent transitions allow stylistic versatility to become
an index of human vitality, and this suggests the major achievement of
the tract: the creation of a rhetorical persona who is an energetic and
imaginative reformer, ready with an appropriate response for every
situation. This wide-ranging literary exuberance and human vitality
of the reformer is in sharp contrast to the Confuter, who has a "coy
flurting stile," and who "makes sentences by the Statute, as if all above
three inches long were confiscat," (I:873). The Confuter's effeminacy
develops in the course of the tract into a systematic denial of life. The
bishops keep the people in superstitious ignorance, denying them their
full human and Christian stature by insisting on set forms of worship
and preventing the dissemination of printed sermons and explanations
of the English Bible: "So little care they of beasts to make them men,
that by their sorcerous doctrine of formalities they take the way to
transforme them out of Christian men into Iudaizing beasts," (I:932).
The Confuter even goes so far as to pervert the life-giving words of
Scripture into a doctrine of worldliness:

> But God incited the wisest man Salomon with these means. Ah

> Confuter of thy selfe, this example hath undone thee, <u>Salomon</u>
> askt an understanding heart, which the Prelats have little care
> to ask. He askt no riches which is their chiefe care: therefore
> was the prayer of <u>Salomon</u> pleasing to God; hee give him wis-
> dome at his request, and riches without asking: as now hee gives
> the Prelats riches at their seeking, and no wisdome because of
> their perverse asking. [I:950]

The vitality of the reformer's persona emerges most clearly in these
direct rebuttals of the Confuter's bland assertions. The reformer
disciplines these glib statements, then transforms them into clearly
articulated truths. In this passage Milton the reformer ascends
through the various worlds that exist in the <u>Apology</u>, from the corrupt
foolishness of the Confuter, to Milton's urbane mockery of his incom-
petence, to a network of lucid antitheses that place Solomon and the
bishops in their sharply opposed worlds, the one in a vital relationship
with truth, the other mired in error.

Nowhere is this method of overwhelming the Confuter's bland es-
pousal of error with the reformer's vitality and understanding better
demonstrated than in Milton's most eloquent statement of disciplined
stylistic freedom:

> But this which comes next in view, I know not what good vein, or
> humour took him, when he let drop into his paper. I that was ere
> while the ignorant, the loyterer, on the sudden by his permission
> am now granted to <u>know something</u>: And that <u>such a volley of ex-
> pressions</u> he hath met withall, <u>as he would never desire to have
> them better cloth'd</u>. For me, Readers, although I cannot say that
> I am utterly untrain'd in those rules which best Rhetoricians have
> giv'n, or unacquainted with those examples which the prime au-
> thors of eloquence have written in any learned tongu, yet true elo-
> quence I find to be none, but the serious and hearty love of truth:
> And that whose mind so ever is fully possest with a fervent desire
> to know good things, and with the dearest charity to infuse the
> knowledge of them into others, when such a man would speak, his
> words (by what I can expresse) like so many nimble and airy ser-
> vitors trip about him at command, and in well order'd files, as he
> would wish, fall aptly into their own places. [I:948–49]

Again we have the reformer moving easily from the urbane, satiric
mode into high eloquence. Fast-paced simple sentences, quoting the
strange half-human Confuter and picturing him in all his ineptitude,
yield to one copious assertion of the nature of truly eloquent rhetoric.
First, in the subordinate clause, Milton recasts the Confuter's pert
rhetorical doctrine into a respectful bow to neoclassic rhetorical
principles. He then sharply transcends this doctrine in the main

clause, a clear assertion of principle: "yet true eloquence I find to be none, but the serious and hearty love of truth." In the additional long, loose dependent clause, he passes through further enumeration of the qualifications for eloquence into a brisk vision of the intellectual and moral power Milton believes reformed man is capable of sustaining: "a fervent desire to know good things . . . the dearest charity . . . when such a man would speak, his words . . . like so many nimble and airy servitors trip about him at command, and in well order'd files, as he would wish, fall aptly into their own places." The two sets of subordinate clauses image the disciplined energy that is needed to bring about reform. This energy is then released into the clear understanding of the main clause and the effortlessly free order described in the conclusion of the long, loose clause. This passage is useful for two further reasons: First, as a celebration of eloquence it corresponds to the visions of poetry in The Reason of Church Government and tends to confirm my suspicion that in the Apology Milton is beginning to esteem prose rhetoric as much as he does poetry. Second, by his manner of dealing with the controversy between himself and the Confuter, Milton absorbs this petty dispute into his own rarefied and lofty universe, exactly as he transposes the events of 1640–1641 into a similarly exalted realm in his address to Parliament.

Joan Webber has said that the Apology "clutches" the reader with aggressive, passionate prose (pp. 203, 205). Certainly it is true that the pamphlet has an impetuous quality; this is partly due to its lack of formal pauses, partly to its stylistic variety. Throughout, the energetic impulses of the reformed and reforming persona are disciplined by a satirical and idealistic imagination, but not by strenuous intellection. Compared to the other antiprelatical tracts, the Apology breaks entirely free of the emotional monomania which dominates Of Reformation and pushes the rather alien intellectual position of The Reason of Church Government into the background by the simple expedient of assuming its truth. We shall witness in the next series of tracts Milton's coming of age as a social thinker; he will supplement imaginative emotions and ideals with vigorous argument and will communicate for the first and last time a social vision which appears to dignify and accommodate the entire English polity and society within its spacious dimensions.

THE DIVORCE TRACTS AND AREOPAGITICA

"The Doctrine and Discipline of Divorce"
and "Tetrachordon"

"About Whitsuntide" of 1642, not long after the Apology was published, Milton "took a journey into the country, nobody about him certainly knowing the reason, or that it was any more than a journey of recreation; after a month's stay, home he returns a married man that went out a bachelor, his wife being Mary, the eldest daughter of Mr. Richard Powell, then a Justice of Peace, of Forest Hill, near Shotover in Oxfordshire."[1] One month later, Mary Powell Milton visited her family at Forest Hill and subsequently refused to return to her husband. The divorce pamphlets were a "direct result" of this unfortunate union.[2] The first of these pamphlets, The Doctrine and Discipline of Divorce, was published in August 1643, and was followed by a greatly revised and augmented second edition in February 1644. To Milton's chagrin, the strenuous rhetorical labors he performed in the two versions of this tract aroused nothing but hostility on the part of the godly and learned men with whom he had allied against the bishops. This remained true even after he had buttressed his position with The [licensed] Judgement of Martin Bucer concerning Divorce. He responded in March 1645 with Tetrachordon, the final version of his argument.

Barker is certainly correct in saying that Milton's disastrous marital experience forced him to "recognize his own humanity" and to argue accordingly in the divorce tracts on behalf of "the legitimate (if frail) inclinations of human nature" (p. 66). He was compelled to become more realistic, to urge greater flexibility on those in charge of society's domestic institutions. Similarly, the absence of unambiguous scriptural support for his views meant that his style had to conform to given human standards of discourse. Again in Barker's words, intellectual necessity drove Milton to think "less zealously and more logically" (pp. 67, 72). And in some ways Milton made a virtue of necessity, integrating logical and pathetic proofs more fully than he had ever done in the antiprelatical tracts and thereby making the arguments on divorce more attractive and powerful as works of rhetorical imagination. Milton's syntax remains nevertheless elaborately and intricately formed. This means that the divorce tracts differ only in degree from the antiprelatical tracts and that they like the antiprelatical tracts, differ in kind from the Leveller prose I have used as a standard of comparison in my first chapter. The sentences continue to call attention to themselves as well-wrought verbal monuments, so that divorce is considered in a literary context which, the more it feels exclusively literary and intellectual, the less it can correspond plausibly and pervasively to recognizable social and domestic contexts. It is only the rhetorical persona who is here made more realistically human; he still inhabits an idealized, ideational world.

Milton's prose advances in these tracts on "domestic liberty" beyond the works on "ecclesiastical liberty" by expressing a fuller range of emotions, as well as by integrating rational and emotional appeals more effectively. The following passage, really a summary of Milton's entire position, forms a major part of what becomes the preface to the second edition of The Doctrine and Discipline:

> What thing more instituted to the solace and delight of man then marriage, and yet the mis-interpreting of some Scripture directed mainly against the abusers of the Law for divorce giv'n by Moses, hath chang'd the blessing of matrimony not seldome into a familiar and co-inhabiting mischiefe; at least into a drooping and disconsolate houshold captivitie, without refuge or redemption . . . . For although God in the first ordaining of marriage, taught us to what end he did it, in words expresly implying the apt and cheerfull conversation of man with woman, to comfort and refresh him against the evill of solitary life, not mentioning the purpose of generation till afterwards, as being but a secondary end in dignitie, though not in necessitie; yet now, if any two be but once handed in the Church, and have tasted in any sort the nuptiall bed, let them finde themselves never so mistak'n in their dispositions through any error, concealment, or misadventure, that through their different tempers, thoughts, and constitutions, they can neither be to one another a remedy against lonelines, nor live in any union or contentment all their dayes, yet they shall, so they be but found suitably weapon'd to the lest possibilitie of sensuall enjoyment, be made, spight of antipathy to fadge together, and combine as they may to their unspeakable wearisomnes & despaire of all sociable delight in the ordinance which God establisht to that very end. [II:235–36]

The first of these two sentences, up to the ellipsis, is a low-keyed rehearsal for the drama to be fully performed in the second sentence. In both sentences God establishes marital paradise and man perversely falls, but in the first sentence the tale is told relatively dispassionately. The attentive reader will, however, respond to the undertones

of melancholy present even here. A paradise of directness and simplicity is complicated by an apparently innocuous intellectual mis-
take, and before man knows it, he is damned, caught in a situation
"without refuge or redemption." This loss of paradise is made to
seem all the more unnecessary and grievous by the way the governing
syntax of the second clause carelessly overrides the correct interpretation of the scriptural passage in question: "and yet the mis-
interpreting of some Scripture directed mainly against the abusers of
the Law for divorce giv'n by Moses, hath chang'd the blessing of matrimony not seldome into a familiar and co-inhabiting mischiefe." One
other subtle and understated little pattern contributes to the gathering
sense of melancholy. In the first clause, social institutions and their
purposes are subservient to man: "What thing more instituted to the
solace and delight of man then marriage" (my emphasis). In the second part of the sentence, two different abstract nouns, "mischiefe"
and "captivitie" have replaced "solace" and "delight" and appear to
name the purposes of existing Canon Law marriage. But these nouns
do more than obliterate the ends of Christian marriage; they abolish
man himself, for their adjectives modify them in such a way that they
appear to be the only inhabitants in the households of ill-matched men
and women: "a familiar and co-inhabiting mischiefe . . . a drooping
and disconsolate houshold captivitie." There even seems to be a
progression in suggested emotional lassitude between the first and the
second of these baroque phrases.

If this overstates the emotional texture so far, it is difficult to ex-
aggerate the impact of the second massive sentence. The irony of its
initial subordinate clause, "For although . . . necessitie," is that it is
a subordinate clause at all and not a self-contained truth. Considered
in itself, the clause both moves fluently towards progressively richer
definition ("the apt and cheerfull conversation of man with woman, to
comfort and refresh him . . .") and rounds itself off by firmly establishing priorities and values ("a secondary end in dignitie, though not
in necessitie"). By these means the reader is invited not only to learn
what marriage is from the best of all possible teachers, but to experience it by savoring the freedom and delight guaranteed by order and
structure. But of course the prefatory "For although" does its work
before any of these effects can be wrought, making the reader anticipate the "yet now" he immediately discovers before he can assimilate
the good news. God's institution has been maliciously subordinated to
man's fallen appetite for narrow and superficial literal-mindedness.

Read in isolation, the primary grammatical elements of the passage
following "yet now" show that the minimum sufficient condition for a
valid marriage according to the Canon Law, a public ceremony, is in
fact only a disguise for the reality of enforced endurance of mechani-

cal sexual coupling: "yet now, if any two be but once handed in the Church, and have tasted in any sort the nuptiall bed, . . . they shall, so they be but found suitably weapon'd to the lest possibilitie of sensuall enjoyment, be made . . . to fadge together." The decorous phrasing of the clause describing the wedding ceremony is first mocked by "tasted in any sort the nuptiall bed," turned into sarcasm in "so they be but found suitably weapon'd," and stripped away in the brutally direct predicate "be made . . . to fadge together." In relation to Canon Law marriage, complex formal syntax thus exists to have its falsity exposed by a few simple and straightforward monosyllables. This is the "main clause" of Canon Law marriage, with the elements emphasized by their separation from each other: "they shall . . . be made . . . to fadge together." A godly institution has been reduced to these rough growls. The indignation of this main clause stands out all the more sharply against the mournful background of the clauses and phrases surrounding it. Before it, the clauses move fluently from one unhappy triplet to the answering rhythm of another ("through any error, concealment, or misadventure . . . through their different tempers, thoughts, and constitutions") and then to the near symmetry of the hopeless conclusions: "they can neither be to one another a remedy against lonelines, nor live in any union or contentment all their dayes." These poised fluencies and harmonies merely emphasize the pain a lifeless marriage causes a man of sensibility. The coordinate extension which follows hard upon the main clause continues to embody the disastrous consequences of tyrannically imposed marriage for an idealistic sensibility: "and combine as they may to their unspeakable wearisomnes & despaire of all sociable delight in the ordinance which God establisht to that very end." Thus the main clause of Canon Law marriage simply tramples on the sensitive man's pain and reduces him at last to a sexual automaton ("and combine as they may"). Milton achieves here something for him entirely new: he confronts a social injustice not just with fiery outrage, but with the entire range of emotions one might expect of a humane reformer, with weary sadness and sarcasm as well as with saeva indignatio. He orchestrates these emotions into coherent and powerful utterance and thus develops his affective posture from an expression of private needs and demands into a communication of public urgencies.[3]

Within the main body of each tract, integrations of logical and pathetic proofs occur more frequently than do polemics of the sort analyzed in the passage above, which depend primarily on a diverse emotional appeal. The following forms part of the exposition of the Mosaic divorce law in Tetrachordon:

> But in Mariage a league of love and willingnes, if faith bee not
> willingly kept, it scars is worth the keeping; nor can bee any de-
> light to a generous minde, with whom it is forcibly kept: and the
> question still supposes the one brought to an impossibility of
> keeping it as hee ought, by the others default, and to keep it for-
> mally, not only with a thousand shifts and dissimulations, but with
> open anguish, perpetual sadnes and disturbance, no willingnes, no
> cheerfulnes, no contentment, cannot bee any good to a minde not
> basely poor and shallow, with whom the contract of love is so
> kept. [II:624-25]

A negative syllogism is half-concealed in the initial assertion. All
true marriages are defined by "willingnes" between man and wife. A
given marriage lacks this definitive quality. It is therefore no true
marriage and "scars is worth the keeping." The rest of the passage
explores the emotional consequences of this conclusion. Each clause
takes off from the notion of "keeping" a dead covenant, on which the
preceding clause is predicated, and each portrays this notion in increasingly somber terms. Thus logical and emotional momentums
are combined. Logic of a kind is pursued further in the next two
clauses, "nor can bee any delight . . . and the question still supposes,"
which examine the consequences of such hollow observances for each
marital partner. At this point pathetic proof begins more fully to
complement quasi-logical proof, for the final clause, while it simply
repeats what has just been demonstrated, also amplifies its emotional
force. I say complements instead of supplants because this fragment
has a rounded logical unity: "and to keep it formally . . . cannot bee
any good to a minde not basely poor and shallow, with whom the contract of love is so kept." Within these boundaries, however, the logic
of dead marriage develops into the crushing logic of daily emptiness
and melancholy: "not only with a thousand shifts and dissimulations,
but with open anguish, perpetual sadnes and disturbance, no willingnes,
no cheerfulnes, no contentment . . . ." There seems to be no way for
the unhappily married man to avoid coming to profound grief. This
sad fact is given the status of an irreversible psychological law by
the rhythmic momentum of the governing construction ("not only . . .
but . . .") and by the steady proliferation of distressing emotional circumstances, increasing from one ("open anguish") to two ("perpetual
sadnes and disturbance") to three ("no willingnes, no cheerfulnes, no
contentment").

   This kind of poised appeal to both the mind and heart is developed
in a more urgent and declamatory fashion towards the end of The
Doctrine and Discipline:

> Now if it be plain that a Christian may be brought into unworthy

bondage, and his religious peace not only interrupted now and
then, but perpetually and finally hinderd in wedlock by mis-yoking
with a diversity of nature as well as of religion, the reasons of
St. Paul [concerning marriage to non-Christians] cannot be made
special to that one case of infidelity, but are of equal moment to
a divorce wherever Christian liberty and peace are without fault
equally obstructed. That the ordinance which God gave to our
comfort, may not be pinn'd upon us to our undeserved thraldom;
to be coop't up as it were in mockery of wedlock, to a perpetual
betrothed lonelines and discontent, if nothing wors ensue. There
beeing nought els of mariage left between such, but a displeasing
and forc't remedy against the sting of a brute desire; which fleshly accustoming without the souls union and commixture of intellectual delight, as it is rather a soiling then a fulfilling of mariage-
rites, so is it anough to imbase the mettle of a generous spirit,
and sinks him to a low and vulgar pitch of endeavour in all his
actions, or, which is wors, leavs him in a dispairing plight of abject and hard'n'd thoughts: which condition, rather then a good
man should fall into, a man usefull in the service of God and man-
kind, Christ himself hath taught us to dispence with the most
sacred ordinances of his worship; even for a bodily healing to
dispence with that holy & speculative rest of Sabbath; much more
then with the erroneous observance of an ill-knotted mariage for
the sustaining of an overcharg'd faith and perseverance. [II:339]

The passage is the kind of dense and extended statement which is
usually designed in Milton's prose and in these tracts in particular to
silence all objection and demolish all opposition. It seems to exhaust
its emotional energy in each series of clauses only to work itself up
to a keener pitch by passing immediately on to more of the same,
utilizing loose syntactical devices such as absolute participials and
trailing relative pronouns: "There beeing . . . which fleshly accustoming . . . which condition." This mode of utterance resembles that
of the antiprelatical tracts in that it seems to be animated by a belief
that if assertion is energetic enough, it can accomplish just about
anything. It differs from anything in the antiprelatical tracts, however, because it is preceded by a closely argued interpretation of
Saint Paul and followed by some convincing reasoning by analogy.
Moreover, this middle section is based on acute insights into the
psychology of distress, insights which are endowed with a kind of
associative logic by the breathless transitions and by an adroit place-
ment of logical tissue: "as it is rather a soiling . . . so it is anough
to imbase the mettle . . . ." There is also no attempt to pause or
make transitions between the more overtly logical sections at the
beginning and end and the tirade in between. So extended a concatena-

tion of thought and feeling reveals in this instance and others how
isolated and unorthodox Milton's views are. Since he can support
them with nothing but the strength and stridency of his own feelings
and arguments, he must bring those feelings and arguments to bear
in their full force when refuting even the most peripheral of the
counterarguments used by spokesmen for the status quo.[4]

The explication in Tetrachordon of the original institution of marriage in Genesis gives Milton an opportunity to escape for a time from
these polemical pressures. Contemplating Paradise before the Fall,
he can revel unabashedly in matrimonial perfection:

> No mortall nature can endure either in the actions of Religion, or
> study of wisdome, without somtime slackning the cords of intense
> thought and labour: which lest we should think faulty, God himself
> conceals us not his own recreations before the world was built; I
> was, saith the eternall wisdome, dayly his delight, playing alwayes
> before him. And to him indeed wisdom is as a high towr of plea-
> sure, but to us a steep hill, and we toyling ever about the bottom:
> he executes with ease the exploits of his omnipotence, as easie as
> with us it is to will: but no worthy enterprise can be don by us
> without continuall plodding and wearisomnes to our faint and sen-
> sitive abilities. We cannot therefore alwayes be contemplative,
> or pragmaticall abroad, but have need of som delightful intermis-
> sions, wherin the enlarg'd soul may leav off a while her severe
> schooling; and like a glad youth in wandring vacancy, may keep
> her hollidaies to joy and harmles pastime: which as she cannot
> well doe without eompany, so in no company so well as where the
> different sexe in most resembling unlikenes, and most unlike re-
> semblance cannot but please best and be pleas'd in the aptitude of
> that variety. Whereof lest we should be too timorous, in the aw
> that our flat sages would form us and dresse us, wisest Salomon
> among his gravest Proverbs contenances a kinde of ravishment
> and erring fondnes in the entertainment of wedded leisures; and
> in the Song of Songs, which is generally beleev'd, even in the
> jolliest expressions to figure the spousals of the Church with
> Christ, sings of a thousand raptures between those two lovely
> ones farre on the hither side of carnall enjoyment. [II:596–97]

A phrase near the begging of the passage, "somtime slackning the
cords of intense thought and labour," summarizes pretty well what is
going on here. Yet this beautiful and lofty presentation is not without
its appeal to reason. The initial claim is immediately supported by
the most authoritative evidence: "God himself conceals us not his
own recreations before the world was built." An axiomatic contrast

is then assuredly tossed off: "He executes with ease . . . but no
worthy enterprise can be don by us without continuall plodding and
wearisomnes." In some genuine and important sense, Milton has
adequately prepared for and can justify the logical tissue binding
together the central point of the passage: "We cannot therefore al-
wayes be contemplative, or pragmaticall abroad, . . . which as she
cannot well doe without company, so in no company so well as where
the different sexe in most resembling unlikenes, and most unlike resemblance cannot but please best and be pleas'd in the aptitude of that
variety" (my emphasis). But this "argument" exploits logic in order
to transcend it. The conclusion that the marital relationship is
uniquely delightful and refreshing succeeds in hailing wedded love,
for it is articulated with an ease which I can only further characterize
by invoking another impressionistic label, fluent balance. This elu-
sive quality of syntax and style is what gives the passage its tone of
untroubled pleasure. Serenity is itself transcended and replaced by
ecstacy in one of the loosely appended amplifying statements Milton
seems always to have at hand: "Whereof lest . . . carnall enjoyment."
By calling on Proverbs and the Song of Songs for substantiation, Milton
continues to the end to provide evidence and to interpret it in a way
that ought to be credible to any rational believer. But above all the
free shape of this climactic syntax generates a joyous dialectic of order and energy: the false order of the "flat sages" who "would form
us and dresse us" in timorous awe is superseded by a juxtaposition
of true order and true energy when "wisest Salomon among his gravest
Proverbs" gives his approval to "a kinde of ravishment and erring
fondnes in the entertainment of wedded leisures." Juxtaposition becomes the harmonious marriage wrought by music in the last and
loveliest predication, which distills the entire discussion into a lilting
cadence: "and in the Song of Songs, . . . sings of a thousand raptures
between those two lovely ones farre on the hither side of carnall enjoyment." Deafeningly polemical passages such as those previously
analyzed exist for the sake of such raptures, which Milton succeeds in
recreating even as he talks about them. William Haller's conclusion
that the divorce tracts are imaginative as well as discursive and logical is absolutely correct.[5] Most emphatically, the way in which Milton's prose rhetoric here integrates logical and pathetic proofs does
lift daily domestic experience up into a higher and better imagined
universe.

    As earlier suggested in passing, the style of these works is gov-
erned by an awareness of how thoroughly unconventional are the views
they espouse: "many truths now of reverend esteem and credit, had
their birth and beginning once from singular and private thoughts;

while the most of men were otherwise possest" (II:241). The attempt
to appeal to both thought and feeling, by and large successful, I would
say, is designed to guard against the easy and cheap accusation that
Milton is merely indulging a private humor or obsession when he
repeatedly imagines that a mistaken marriage can be a sort of living
death.[6] The structure of each tract has a similar purpose. Barker's
comments are once again helpful: "Milton's mind sweeps out from
the centre of discussion in ever-widening circles, and each argument
is supported by increasingly broader applications" (p. 110). In the
first edition of The Doctrine and Discipline, however, this intellectual
rhythm is left unclear. The division into books and chapters in the
second edition brings it out into the open, replacing the sense of impetuous debate found in the first edition with a sense of mature consideration. Specifically, the chapter titles added in the second edition
provide the tract with the apparatus of sober, painstaking argument.
The treatise becomes the laborious construction of an intellectual order, until divorce for reasons more dignified than adultery finds its
rightful place among a body of accepted, certified public truths. The
procedure of the first book is less systematic than that of the second.
Milton simply interprets the Mosaic Law and lists a number of prag-
matic reasons in favor of divorce for "unfitnes and defectivenes of an
unconjugal mind." Each chapter is by itself a proof of Milton's view.
Marriage laws should be less concerned with the state of a man's
body, more with his mind and spirit. The Canon Law prohibition of
divorce is a temptation to the unhappily married Christian to despair.
This prohibition violates nature by preventing people naturally averse
to each other from separating. Many of these chapters simply repeat
the same arguments in different terms (for instance, chapters 2, 3, 4,
9, 12, and 13). The effect is that in the first book, rhetorical impetus
is provided by the disciplined emotional energy of Milton's private
marital vision, which grabs haphazardly at any rational support it can
find. By suggesting that there must be some truth in Milton's contentions, these confident but slightly disorganized proofs erode by a
flanking movement the reader's defenses, which are based upon the
apparent and literal meaning of Christ's response to the Pharisees in
Matthew 19:3—9.
    The second book moves in a more strictly logical way through an
exposition of the Mosaic divorce law and its Pauline relation to the
Gospel. Greatly expanded in the second edition, this exposition
amounts to an extended syllogism: The Mosaic law, because it was
the Law, could not have been a permission to sin; it was a valid attempt to rescue from the consequences of the Fall the purpose named
in the original institution of marriage, fit "conversation" between male
and female. Since the Gospel is more charitable towards legitimate

instincts than was the Law, Christ could not have meant to abrogate
this particularly charitable law when he answered the Pharisees'
question; he was merely rebuking them for their abuse of divorce.
Therefore the divorcing of marriages which fail to achieve fit conversation is entirely proper in a Christian society. In the second
book, the reader's defenses are methodically destroyed by elaborate
and ingenious logic. By the time he reaches the weak link in Milton's
massive syllogism, the interpretation of Christ's answer to the Pharisees, he has nothing to put up against it but the bare literal meaning
of the text. He _must_ see, so this slow passionate movement entreats,
that this literal meaning clearly disagrees with all that a humane
Christian society knows to be true. Thus Milton's private humor, his
vision of married loneliness, is vindicated by a structure of Christian
truth which provides a remedy for such loneliness. It is the Canonists,
their faculties so obscured and distorted by custom that they think Law
can be sinful and Grace stricter than Law, who are violating this public
structure and pursuing a perverse humor: "but if the perfect, the pure,
the righteous law of God, for so are all his statutes and his judgements,
be found to have allow'd smoothly without any certain reprehension,
that which Christ afterward declares to be adultery, how can wee free
this Law from the horrible endightment of beeing both impure, unjust,
and fallacious" (II:284). The thrust of the treatise as a whole exactly
parallels what we have seen to be Milton's consistent tendency. It
labors to elevate English marital customs into an ideal order, to show
that a charitable divorce law ought to be "suffer'd to stand in the place
where God set it amidst the firmament of his holy Laws to shine, as it
was wont, upon the weaknesses and errors of men perishing els in the
sincerity of their honest purposes" (II:351).

As Ernest Sirluck demonstrates, in Tetrachordon Milton tried to
strengthen his crucial argument:

> [God] suffer'd his owne people to wast and spoyl and slay by warre,
> to lead captives, to be som maisters, som servants, som to be
> princes, others to be subjects, hee suffer'd propriety to divide all
> things by severall possession, trade and commerce, not without
> usury; in his common wealth some to bee undeservedly rich, others
> to be undeservingly poore. All which till hardnesse of heart came
> in, was most unjust; whenas prime Nature made us all equall, made
> us equall coheirs by common right and dominion over all creatures.
> In the same manner, and for the same cause hee suffer'd divorce
> as well as mariage, our imperfet and degenerat condition of neces-
> sity requiring this law among the rest, as a remedy against intol-
> erable wrong and servitude above the patience of man to beare.[7]
> [II:661]

This is the essence of a new interpretation of the phrase "for your hardness of heart" in Christ's answer to the Pharisees. It still refers to the accidental, unavoidable sufferance of evil through abuse of a good law by bad men. But now it also refers to the fallen condition of all men, and it implies that the Mosaic divorce law is one of the "secondary laws of nature" framed by God to make allowances for the Fall. In the parliamentary apologies that appeared during the period between the second edition of The Doctrine and Discipline and Tetrachordon, this concept of a secondary Law of Nature had been used to justify rebellion against tyranny, and Sirluck concludes that Milton simply lifted it from these apologetics and applied it to the question of divorce (PW, II:153–58).

The importance of this new argument for our purposes, however, is that it coincides with a new rhetorical arrangement. It is a direct link between Milton's general position and God's plan for mitigating the consequences of the Fall. Throughout the tract, the strict exegetical structure suggests this kind of link. To expound "upon the foure chief places in Scripture, which treat of mariage, or nullities in mariage" is to prove one's views by tracing the history of God's efforts to rescue man from the Fall. This structure, both logically strict and, as we shall see, imaginatively suggestive, constitutes a network of defenses stronger than that in The Doctrine and Discipline against the telling objection from the literal meaning of Christ's answer to the Pharisees. That literal meaning sounds out as a barbarous dissonance from the harmony of sacred history, which the reader has heard chiming in the Mosaic Law even after the Fall. Christ was the fulfillment of sacred history: God did not send him into the world to wander off on a wild tangent from it. Therefore he must have been speaking of the secondary Law of Nature when he answered the Pharisees. Milton's interpretation allows the text to fall neatly into place in a historical myth which all Christians should accept. In short, all the arguments of The Doctrine and Discipline are incorporated into a clearer, more assured pattern of divine actions, by which marriage is instituted in full perfection and restored as far as possible by lawgiving and Grace. The obstinately literal Canonist stands more lucidly and urbanely accused of violating the harmonies of divine benevolence.

The exegetical narrative is interrupted only once, after the exposition of the original institution of marriage in Genesis. By Aristotelian causal analysis, Milton draws together the results of his contemplation of Paradise: "Mariage is a divine institution joyning man and woman in a love fitly dispos'd to the helps and comforts of domestic life" (II: 612). This definition provides a focus for the entire debate on divorce. It recollects the truth about marriage into one lucid sentence and thus

suggests a way to set at least one social institution in accord with
God's benevolence. This moment of clarity, poised between Paradise
and history, produces a rational image of unfallen marriage which
will be pieced together again and again in the course of history after
the Fall by Moses, Christ, Saint Paul, Fathers and Reformers, and
finally by Milton himself. The tract thus seeks not a harmony between
four passages of Scripture so much as a harmony between contemporary social institutions and the grand pattern of sacred history adumbrated in those four passages. The exegetical format functions as a
kind of systematic metaphor, a background narration of the evolution
of God's generous vision for humanity, against which the restrictive-
ness of the Canon Law is projected and fully exposed. Even more so
than in The Doctrine and Discipline, this structure seeks to absorb
patterns of daily life into the one true ideal universe.
   Milton complained of the neglect and misunderstanding suffered by
his works on divorce:

> I did but prompt the age to quite their cloggs
> By the known rules of ancient libertie,
> When strait a barbarous noise environs me
> Of Owles and Cuckoes, Asses, Apes, and Doggs . . .
> That bawle for freedom in their senceless mood
> And still revolt when truth would set them free.
> Licence they mean when they cry libertie.
>   [Sonnet XII]

I must once again stress that this immediate political failure was entirely predictable, and for two reasons besides the fact that Milton's
views were so radical: First, the idealistic cast of Milton's imagination leads him into false, or at least extreme, portrayals of domestic
experience. He repeatedly and vividly juxtaposes proffered marital
bliss with the likelihood of marital hell, thereby depriving the reader
of any rhetorical experience of a daily domestic context, the only context in which Milton's proposed reforms would be meaningful. Second,
Milton appears to believe that fully exploiting the resources of language can by itself produce social change. In two years' time he published three major treatises arguing for radical revisions in divorce
laws, not to mention an auxiliary work marshaling the like-minded
views of a respected reformer. Each treatise is "wov'n close, both
matter, form and stile" (Sonnet XI), filled with one massive sentence
after another battering away at the inertial resistance of custom and
received opinion. To suppose that words alone can have such impact,
to work so hard and so repetitiously at envisioning daily life in such
an imaginatively colored and intensified perspective, is to continue
to ignore or misconceive the imperatives of political action and to
write not pamphlets but poems.

"Areopagitica"

They are nevertheless good poems, and in the interim between The
Doctrine and Discipline and Tetrachordon Milton wrote an even better
one. Areopagitica, published 23 November 1644, was a direct result
of Milton's advocacy of reformed divorce laws. In a sermon preached
on 13 August 1644 before a joint audience of Parliament and the Westminster Assembly, a leading member of the Assembly, Herbert Palmer, demanded that Milton's unlicensed "wicked booke" on divorce "be
burnt" (this must have referred to The Doctrine and Discipline, since
The Judgement of Martin Bucer had been licensed). On 26 August,
the House of Commons referred to its Committee for Printing a peti-
tion from the Stationers Company and instructed the committee "dili-
gently to inquire out the Authors, Printers, and Publishers of the
Pamphlet against the Immortality of the Soul, and concerning Divorce."[8] Although it appears that these attacks resulted in no action
against Milton, they must have convinced him that his former allies
against the bishops were no friends to free inquiry and free speech.
At the urging of learned acquaintances, therefore, Milton decided to
argue for the abrogation of a law of Parliament which he felt would
be a dangerous weapon in the hands of Presbyterian and other bigots,
the Licensing Ordinance of 14 June 1643.[9] In the ensuing oration, the
rhetorical methods we have seen developing through Milton's earlier
work all come to fruition. Argumentative vigor becomes inseparable
from imaginative vitality, and emotional appeals achieve a new range
and urbanity. The agile voice of the Apology, intellectually and imaginatively disciplined by the experience of the first three divorce
tracts, becomes a humanly appealing persona, fully qualified to communicate a progressive social vision.[10]

One characteristic of this persona is his flexible and poised command of emotions. The discussions of pagan culture at the beginning
of the tract, which establish Milton's credentials as a man of wide and
deep learning, are written in a style of loose and chatty antiquarian-
ism reminiscent of Browne:

> Neither is it recorded that the writings of those old Comedians
> were supprest, though the acting of them were forbid; and that
> Plato commended the reading of Aristophanes the loosest of them
> all, to his royal scholler Dionysius, is commonly known, and may
> be excus'd, if holy Chrysostome, as is reported, nightly studied
> so much the same Author and had the art to cleanse a scurrilous
> vehemence into the stile of a rousing Sermon. . . .
> The Romans also for many ages train'd up only to a military
> roughnes, resembling most the Lacedaemonian guise, knew of

> learning little but what their twelve Tables, and the <u>Pontifick</u>
> College with their <u>Augurs</u> and <u>Flamins</u> taught them in Religion
> and Law, so unacquainted with other learning, that when <u>Car</u>-
> <u>neades</u> and <u>Critolaus</u>, with the <u>Stoick Diogenes</u> comming Em-
> bassadors to <u>Rome</u>, tooke thereby occasion to give the City a
> tast of their Philosophy, they were suspected for seducers by no
> lesse a man then <u>Cato</u> the Censor, who mov'd it in the Senat to
> dismisse them speedily, and to banish all such <u>Attick</u> bablers out
> of <u>Italy</u>. But <u>Scipio</u> and others of the noblest Senators withstood
> him and his old <u>Sabin</u> austerity; honour'd and admir'd the men;
> and the Censor himself at last in his old age fell to the study of
> that whereof before hee was so scrupulous. [II:495–96, 497–98]

Of course, passages such as these demonstrate that Milton's knowledge of the Western tradition is both thorough and affectionate. They
further suggest in two ways the importance of liberalizing censorship.
First, evidently even a man who likes nothing so much as to peruse
old books has felt compelled to take up the cause of freedom for new
books. Second, if there was little censorship in such relaxed and easy-
going cultures as those of antiquity, it is all the more important that
censorship be kept to a minimum after Christianity and the Reformation have transformed the world, after the reentry of Truth into the
world has made every subsequent true discovery eternally significant.

This relaxed mood is replaced by more varied emotions when
Milton considers the history of censorship in the Christian era and
proceeds to his main arguments for abolition of the Licensing Ordinance. The tonal change reinforces the change in subject from relative classical innocence to mature Christian experience. The gentle
humanist scholar is reborn as the crusading Protestant, who is nevertheless as prone to sensitive grief as is his brother in the divorce
tracts:

> Truth indeed came once into the world with her divine Master,
> and was a perfect shape most glorious to look on: but when he
> ascended, and his Apostles after him were laid asleep, then
> strait arose a wicked race of deceivers, who as that story goes
> of the <u>AEgyptian Typhon</u> with his conspirators, how they dealt
> with the good <u>Osiris</u>, took the virgin Truth, hewd her lovely form
> into a thousand peeces, and scatter'd them to the four winds.
> From that time ever since, the sad friends of Truth, such as
> durst appear, imitating the carefull search that <u>Isis</u> made for
> the mangl'd body of <u>Osiris</u>, went up and down gathering up limb
> by limb still as they could find them. [II:549]

When he speaks as the true warfaring Christian, it is with an aware-

ness of the excessive zeal and emerging fanaticism of his own former
friends:

> And in their name I shall for neither friend nor foe conceal what
> the generall murmur is; that if it come to inquisitioning again,
> and licencing, and that we are so timorous of our selvs, and so
> suspicious of all men, as to fear each book, and the shaking of
> every leaf, before we know what the contents are, if some who
> but of late were little better then silenc't from preaching, shall
> come now to silence us from reading, except what they please, it
> cannot be guest what is intended by som but a second tyranny over
> learning: and will soon put it out of controversie that Bishops and
> Presbyters are the same to us both name and thing. [II:539]

This passage is more tightly structured and carefully developed than
any of the polemical salvos we have seen heretofore. It builds and
intensifies through a series of subordinate and conditional clauses,
but resolves itself with a sharp and witty finality instead of extending
itself indefinitely in a chain of loose amplifying clauses. The effect
is that zeal and righteousness are confined and controlled, kept in
their polemical place in order to save rhetorical energies for more
positive purposes.

Subordinating zeal to other rhetorical imperatives is one of the
aspects of Areopagitica which make it unique in Milton's political
prose. The oration also achieves insights into the limitations of
zeal:

> No musick must be heard, no song be set or sung, but what is
> grave and Dorick. There must be licencing dancers, that no ges-
> ture, motion, or deportment be taught our youth but what by their
> allowance shall be thought honest; for such Plato was provided of;
> It will ask more then the work of twenty licencers to examin all
> the lutes, the violins, and the ghittarrs in every house; they must
> not be suffer'd to prattle as they doe, but must be licenc'd what
> they may say. And who shall silence all the airs and madrigalls,
> that whisper softnes in chambers? The Windows also, and the
> Balcone's must be thought on, there are shrewd books, with dan-
> gerous Frontispices set to sale; who shall prohibit them, shall
> twenty licencers? The villages also must have their visitors to
> enquire what lectures the bagpipe and the rebbeck reads ev'n to
> the ballatry, and the gammuth of every municipal fidler, for
> these are the Countrymans Arcadia's and his Monte Mayors.
> Next, what more Nationall corruption, for which England hears
> ill abroad, then houshold gluttony; who shall be the rectors of
> our daily rioting? and what shall be done to inhibit the multitudes
> that frequent those houses where drunk'nes is sold and harbour'd?

Our garments also should be referr'd to the licencing of some
more sober work-masters to see them cut into a lesse wanton
garb. Who shall regulat all the mixt conversation of our youth,
male and female together, as is the fashion of this Country, who
shall still appoint what shall be discours'd, what presum'd, and
no furder? Lastly, who shall forbid and separat all idle resort,
all evill company? These things will be, and must be; but how
they shall be lest hurtfull, how lest enticing, herein consists the
grave and governing wisdom of a State. [II:523–26]

Milton writing simple sentences is something we have not seen before and will not see again. So many such sentences coming one after
another reveal the grotesque proportions of a censored society. Each
brief statement shows the uprising of a new manifestation of dangerous
human energies, and their relentless accumulation implies that the
social policy of the Presbyterians must be nothing but an absurdly
frantic and continuous repression. No sooner is one perilous tendency
beaten down than another springs up in its place. The concluding sentence is noticeably more rounded in its form and measured in its pace,
suggesting a wiser and more dignified society in which human vitality
is tempered rather than stifled.

The discipline and urbanity evident throughout Areopagitica generate an emotional texture which transcends sentimentality and hysteria. Such self-control also produces flexible modulations of tone.
An eloquent summary can be rounded off with a homely joke: "And
he who were pleasantly dispos'd, could not well avoid to lik'n it to the
exploit of that gallant man who thought to pound up the crows by
shutting his Parkgate" (II:520). All these virtues unite in the persona
Milton has created to demonstrate that a man can be passionate in
support of a just cause without losing his civilized poise. In terms
of Milton's own personality, this persona represents a fusion of his
Hebraic and Hellenistic impulses. In terms of contemporary political
and intellectual conflict, the speaker embodies a just balancing of
commitment and detachment, avoiding the intemperate bigotry of a
William Prynne, on the one hand, and the "lukewarme" rationality of
a Bishop Hall, on the other. He is a model for the kind of disciplined
freedom the relaxation of censorship could help to instill in all men.

Except for remarking on some of the ways in which it differs from
Milton's usual style, I have not been analyzing the syntax of Areopagitica as minutely as that of the other tracts. This is due to the fact
that Areopagitica exhibits the "strong ratiocinative progress" K. G.
Hamilton claims Milton's pamphlets normally avoid. Hamilton argues,
correctly, that in a tract by Milton the individual sentence replaces
general structure as the primary rhetorical element.[11] But Areo-

pagitica does have a carefully articulated logical structure. It develops each of its arguments and arranges them in a sequence that
builds towards the one that is most significant and convincing. As
we shall see below, Areopagitica is also blessed with a rich imaginative structure. The analyst's attention is therefore diverted from
sentence form to these larger rhetorical patterns. The passage in-
troducing the tract's ultimate argument also illustrates its unobtrusive syntax:

> Well knows he who uses to consider, that our faith and knowledge
> thrives by exercise, as well as our limbs and complexion. Truth
> is compar'd in Scripture to a streaming fountain; if her waters
> flow not in a perpetuall progression, they sick'n into a muddy
> pool of conformity and tradition. A man may be a heretick in the
> truth; and if he beleeve things only because his Pastor sayes so,
> or the Assembly so determins, without knowing other reason,
> though his belief be true, yet the very truth he holds, becomes
> his heresie. There is not any burden that some would gladlier
> post off to another, then the charge and care of their Religion.
> There be, who knows not that there be of Protestants and pro-
> fessors who live and dye in as arrant an implicit faith, as any
> lay Papist of Loretto. [II:543–44]

Sentence form has here no other function but to facilitate clarity.
Each sentence consists of little beyond direct assertion. Amplification and emphasis are not urgent requirements but simple pleasures.

Thus, the emphasis of measured gravity is provided by the initial
construction, "Well knows he who uses to consider," and by such
interpolations as "There be, who knows not that there be." Thus,
amplification is a matter of restating the previous assertion in a
more leisurely and enriched manner, after a full stop has given the
reader an opportunity fully to apprehend and appreciate that previous assertion. This careful proportioning of simple statement and
slightly more complex explanation leads the reader not only to accept
what is after all a paradox, that "A man may be a heretick in the
truth," but to believe that he is merely being reminded of something
he has always known.
      The aptness and plausibility of the analogical images in the first
two sentences of the passage also contribute to this effect. The way
these images are used, as tools of argument, is typical of the entire
oration.[12] Indeed this particular and climactic argument, that censorship stands in the way of fallen man's most important work, the
recollection of truth, is carried forward almost exclusively by imaginative devices. The images here are followed by three "characters"
of conforming heretics, the mournful allegory of the shattered body of

Truth, and several interpretations of the events since 1640 which are
clearly identified as visions: "Behold now this vast City; . . . Me-
thinks I see in my mind a noble and puissant Nation" (II:553–54,
557–58). Logical conclusion and imaginative climax are thus one and
the same in Areopagitica. To "soare a while as the Poets use" is not
now to digress from the argument, as it was in the antiprelatical
tracts, but to extend and fulfill it.

The structure of the oration can thus be summarily described by
saying that it moves from proper names to local imagery to the more
extended metaphors of character, conceit, allegory, and vision.[13]
The first historical argument, establishing the guilt of censorship by
its association with popery, also establishes a latitude of discourse.
The speaker strolls cheerfully through the Western tradition, pre-
paring the way for the more significant later arguments in which he
will roam imaginatively instead of geographically and historically.
The prose "poetry" which dominates these later sections yields two
arguments more basic and exciting than the surface argumentation,
ingenious and convincing as this is. First, the consistent felicity of
the images and other devices implies that free and disciplined creativity is mobilizing itself in instinctive opposition to its censors and
repressors. That Areopagitica is in fact making this point compellingly I can only substantiate by quoting one of the many passages
that consistently and serenely say what they have to say in metaphoric
language. This particular excerpt appears before any of the overt
arguments and thus announces the significance of the imagination for
all that is to follow:

> For Books are not absolutely dead things, but doe contain a
> potencie of life in them to be as active as that soule was whose
> progeny they are; nay they do preserve as in a violl the purest
> efficacie and extraction of that living intellect that bred them.
> I know they are as lively, and as vigorously productive, as those
> fabulous Dragons teeth; and being sown up and down, may chance
> to spring up armed men. And yet on the other hand unlesse
> warinesse be us'd, as good almost kill a Man as kill a good Book;
> who kills a Man kills a reasonable creature, Gods Image; but hee
> who destroyes a good Booke, kills reason it selfe, kills the Image
> of God, as it were in the eye. Many a man lives a burden to the
> Earth; but a good Booke is the pretious life-blood of a master
> spirit, imbalm'd and treasur'd up on purpose to a life beyond life,
> . . . We should be wary therefore what persecution we raise
> against the living labours of publick men, how we spill that sea-
> son'd life of man preserv'd and stor'd up in Books; since we see
> a kinde of homicide may be thus committed, sometimes a mar-
> tyrdome, and if it extend to the whole impression, a kinde of

massacre, whereof the execution ends not in the slaying of an
elementall life, but strikes at that ethereall and fift essence, the
breath of reason it selfe, slaies an immortality rather then a life.
[II:492–93]

The second of these poetic arguments results from the structure and
is reinforced by the title, which alludes to Saint Paul respectfully but
to Isocrates ironically. Isocrates had demanded stricter controls on
the behavior of Athenians. Saint Paul preached to good news of
Christian liberty to those same Athenians. Milton now exhorts his
countrymen to liberate themselves from external controls altogether
and make Saint Paul's message at long last socially viable. The argument the structure makes as it ascends from history to vision, in
other words, is that if not arrested by censorship, the full reformation of England will be the imaginative climax of Western civilization.[14]

As a work of art, Areopagitica is the most successful of Milton's
prose writings because it is sustained and supported by his belief that
the entire nation is beginning to live up to his high imaginative standards: "For now the time seems come, wherein Moses the great
Prophet may sit in heav'n rejoycing to see that memorable and glorious wish of his fulfill'd, when not only our sev'nty Elders, but all the
Lords people are become Prophets" (II:555–56). Milton imagines
that his words are not alone but are cooperating with the words and
deeds of most other Englishmen. This releases his style from the
need to say everything all at once again and again in one elaborate
sentence after another. In other tracts, the unrelieved succession of
such complex sentences substitutes, finally, for clear images of social
reality. But in Areopagitica variations of tone and syntax are utilized
to permit clear images of a new, more nearly ideal society to shine
forth. The rhetorical result is that we really do come to believe that
good books constitute a universe of intellectual vigor or that London
was once a workshop of Truth. At the very least we come to believe
in these things as indicating a possible future. That the men waging
war and reforming the church were too busy with these more immediate and pressing issues to listen to Milton and imagine with him
was, this one time, the misfortune of the political realities, not of
Milton's rhetoric.[15]

THE ANTIMONARCHICAL TRACTS

"The Tenure of Kings and Magistrates"

Published 13 February 1649, thirteen days after the public execution
of King Charles I, The Tenure of Kings and Magistrates was according
to Masson probably written "mainly while the King was yet being tried,
or was under sentence, and only touched here and there with additions
after his death."[1] Milton had retired from pamphleteering after the
appearance of Tetrachordon and Colasterion in March 1645, disgusted
at the ignorant and abusive reception of his works on divorce by Presbyterian and other narrow minds. During this silence of four years,
he had set down his growing hostility toward the Presbyterians in the
digression entitled "The Character of the Long Parliament and Assembly of Divines" in the third book of his History of Britain, probably written sometime in 1648:

> And yet the main Doctrin for which they took such pay, and in-
> sisted upon with more vehemence than gospel, was but to tell us
> in effect, that their Doctrin was worth nothing, and the Spiritual
> Power of their ministrie less available than Bodilie Compulsion;
> perswading the Magistrate to use it, as a stronger means to sub-
> due and bring in Conscience, than Evangelical perswasion. [V:446]

What Milton had suspected and attacked in the more polemical sections of Areopagitica appeared to be happening. The self-righteous
Presbyterians seemed determined to prevent the imaginative social
quest Milton had foreseen in his great oration and to cut off the free
flow of intellectual and religious inquiry which Milton hoped would
continue recollecting the fragmented body of Truth. Beyond any doubt
Milton looked upon—or convinced himself to look upon—the trial of the
king as a major step in this process, a rediscovery by men of heroic
virtue of the true principle that magistrates are strictly accountable
to the people, from whom all their authority and power derive. Therefore, when the Presbyterian clergy condemned the proceedings against
the king in a multitude of sermons and pamphlets (most notably in the
Serious and Faithfull Representation of the Judgements of Ministers
of the Gospel within the Province of London of 18 January 1649), Milton felt called upon to argue for the truths embodied in that most just
trial.[2]

Had the punishment of the king been a gesture of political dignity
and freedom carried through by a united people, the Tenure might

have been an imaginative celebration of it more eloquent and visionary than <u>Areopagitica</u>. In fact, these unconstitutional proceedings
were a desperate gamble by a few army officers and Independents in
Parliament faced by a crafty enemy and weakened by the splintering
of their own coalition.[3] In these circumstances, Milton's tract had to
be a defense, not a celebration. It had to demolish, as it were, the
obstacles to imaginative social progress which had been erected by
the articulate opposition of the Presbyterians. To do so, it had to
abandon the imaginative method of <u>Areopagitica</u> and revert instead to
the integrated polemical appeals to reason and emotion that had been
developed in the divorce tracts.[4]

     The syllogistic thrust of the <u>Tenure</u> is incisive and penetrating:[5]
"Secondly, that to say, as is usual, the King hath as good right to his
Crown and dignitie, as any man to his inheritance, is to make the
Subject no better then the Kings slave, his chattell, or his possession
that may be bought and sould" (III:203). In compressing the argument,
Milton immediately exposes the commonplace banality ("as is usual")
of royalist thought. The final phrase, "or his possession that may be
bought and sould," exposes also the self-contradictory nature of the
absolutist maxim, for it reveals that the argument devours its own
analogical foundations. If we suppose that "the King hath as good
right to his Crown and dignitie, as any man to his inheritance," we
suppose an absurdity. Either the subject retains his right to his inheritance, in which case he himself is not a "possession that may be
bought and sould" and the king's power is not absolute, or else the
king's power is as absolute as this argument tries vainly to make it,
in which case the subject's right to his inheritance is abrogated.
What is implied here by this self-cannibalizing misuse of reason on
the part of royalists is what will soon become glaringly evident, that
the royalist position is no more than an assertion of arbitrary and
irrational brute force.
     Toying with the tenets of his slipshod opponents, Milton next ima-
gines what this argument based on heredity might mean if taken seriously:

> But suppose it to be of right hereditarie, what can be more just
> and legal, if a subject for certain crimes be to forfet by Law
> from himself, and posterity, all his inheritance to the King, then
> that a King for crimes proportional, should forfet all his title and
> inheritance to the people: unless the people must be thought cre-
> ated all for him, he not for them, and they all in one body inferior
> to him single, which were a kinde of treason against the dignitie
> of mankind to affirm. [III:203-04]

In short, this argument supports the major contentions of the Tenure
when construed reasonably. Both subject and king inherit duties and
responsibilities along with property rights. The foundation of the
state is not conquest but contract, not force but Law. Such a state
achieves an exact rational symmetry in its rewards and punishments:
"a subject for certain crimes be to forfet by Law . . . all his inheritance to the King . . . a King for crimes proportional, should forfet
all his title and inheritance to the people." We are reminded that
there are those working against the establishment of such a political
order by the first appended clause, which emphasizes the gross dis-
proportion of the absolutist state. The second appended clause re-
affirms the axiom of human freedom as the ultimate source of all
refutations of absolutism and refers back to the preceding discussion
of the social contract, which I have explored at length above in the
first chapter.

Milton now gets immediately to the point, the impossibility of
rational foundation or control in an absolute monarchy:

> Thirdly it follows, that to say Kings are accountable to none but
> God, is the overturning of all Law and government. For if they
> may refuse to give account, then all cov'nants made with them at
> Coronation; all Oathes are in vaine, and meer mockeries, all
> Lawes which they sweare to keep, made to no purpose; for if the
> King feare not God, as how many of them doe not? we hold then
> our lives and estates, by the tenure of his meer grace and mercy,
> as from a God, not a mortal Magistrate, a position that none but
> Court Parasites or men besotted would maintain. [III:204]

Since the royalist position remains logically the same but is more
nakedly formulated, Milton's rebuttal is identical to his previous ones
but exposes the calamitous results of political unreason even more
forcefully. Absolutism means a return to the state of warring nature
that prevailed after the Fall: "the overturning of all Law and government." The stricter but no less emphatic logic of the next two sentences vindicates this apparently extreme claim. These sentences
become progressively more specific and derisive in their explications
of "the overturning of all Law and government." The first, its impact
reinforced by rhythmic elaboration, lists what is abrogated by the divine right of kings, "all cov'nants made with them at Coronation; all
Oathes are in vaine, and meer mockeries, all Lawes which they
sweare to keep, made to no purpose." The second, again employing
an "if . . . then" causal construction, shows that the divine right of
kings amounts to blasphemy and is a sign of stupidity or madness in
those who advocate it: "we hold then our lives and estates, by the
tenure of his meer grace and mercy, as from a God, not a mortal
Magistrate, a position that none but Court Parasites or men besotted

would maintain." The final development of this series of arguments is thus to demonstrate that the overturning of legal restraints on a king leads in all probability to the destruction of the rational dignity proper to both subject and king, which means that endorsing absolutist politics is tantamount to embracing a social nightmare:

> And surely no Christian Prince, not drunk with high mind, and prouder then those Pagan Caesars that deifi'd themselves, would arrogate so unreasonably above human condition, or derogate so basely from a whole Nation of men his Brethren, as if for him only subsisting, and to serve his glory; valuing them in comparison of his owne brute will and pleasure, no more then so many beasts, or vermin under his Feet, not to be reasond with, but to be trod on; among whom there might be found so many thousand Men for wisdom, vertue, nobleness of mind, and all other respects, but the fortune of his dignity, farr above him. [III:204–05]

Here we have the disappearance of humanity altogether, the end of mutual dignity and rational communication and their replacement by a self-deified brute trampling on beasts and vermin, with the antisymmetry of this social "order" pointed up by the play on "arrogate . . . derogate." This is the logical result, we are to believe, of the innocuous-seeming banalities so often flowing from the pens of the apologists for King Charles. More so than in the divorce tracts, the Tenure thus builds to a scathing and indignant tone without disturbing its appearance of close argumentation. This stricter integration of reason and emotion is appropriate to polemics aimed at a specific and powerful faction, as opposed to attacks on customs deeply embedded and widespread in the society at large. It is also the first sign of one of the two major stylistic features of Milton's later prose, its tendency to seem more rigorously and formally rational in response to increasing political pressure on Milton's ideals.

When directly attacking the Presbyterian faction, however, Milton dispenses with the subtleties that create the rational surface in order to achieve more titanic expressions of righteous anger. The tract begins by drawing a parallel between custom and political tyranny. Those who allow custom to tyrannize over their lives will welcome external tyranny in the state. This shrewd analysis of the relations between moral dignity and political allegiances is soon applied to current events, as Milton turns to examine the conduct during recent years of certain idolaters of custom:

> And although somtimes for shame, and when it comes to thir owne grievances, of purse especially, they would seeme good Patriots, and side with the better cause, yet when others for the deliverance of thir Countrie, endu'd with fortitude and Heroick vertue to feare

nothing but the curse writt'n against those That doe the worke of
the Lord negligently, would goe on to remove, not only the calamities and thraldoms of a People, but the roots and causes whence
they spring, streight these men, and sure helpers at need, as if
they hated only the miseries but not the mischiefs, after they have
juggl'd and palter'd with the world, bandied and born armes against
thir King, devested him, disannointed him, nay curs'd him all over
in thir Pulpits and thir Pamphlets, to the ingaging of sincere and
real men, beyond what is possible or honest to retreat from, not
only turne revolters from those principles, which only could at
first move them, but lay the staine of disloyaltie, and worse, on
those proceedings, which are the necessary consequences of thir
own former actions; nor dislik'd by themselves, were they manag'd
to the intire advantages of thir own Faction; not considering the
while that he toward whom they boasted thir new fidelitie, counted
them accessory; and by those Statutes and Lawes which they so
impotently brandish against others, would have doom'd them to a
Traytors death, for what they have don alreadie. [III:191–92]

The polemical force of this effusion is threefold: The behavior of
"these men" is plausible in relation to the preceding argument concerning their affinity with tyrants; it is inconsistent and incongruous
when measured against any kind of standard of fidelity to true political
principles; for the same reasons that it is incongruous, it is contemptible and should be condemned by all zealous partisans of truth. A
logical conclusion is made into a rhetorical climax by the density and
length of condemnation. A complex network of delaying suspensions,
which surrounds and separates the elements of the central predication, both establishes the rational standard of heroic consistency and
builds up a store of zealous polemical energies by its length and amplitude. The passage tantalizes the reader and the Presbyterians with
the beginning of the resolving assertion, "streight these men, and sure
helpers at need," then builds up more energies with additional suspensions: "as if they hated . . . after they have . . . to the ingaging of . . . ."
These clauses further increase the rational and emotional pressures on
the Presbyterians, the emotional pressures in particular by a staccato
sequence of verbs: "juggl'd and palter'd with the world, bandied and
born armes against thir King, devested him, disannointed him, nay
curs'd him." So much force has by now been mobilized that the major
predication cannot adequately release and resolve it, and the passage
spills over into one loose amplifier after another: "not only turne
revolters . . . which only could . . . but lay the staine of disloyaltie,
and worse, on those proceedings, which are the necessary consequences . . . nor dislik'd . . . were they manag'd to the . . . advantages
of thir own Faction; not considering . . . that he toward whom they

boasted . . . and by those Statutes . . . which they so impotently brandish . . . would have doom'd them to a Traytors death." In terms of
the traditional Ciceronian metaphors, the closed fist of logic and zeal
strikes at the Presbyterian menace with what is meant to be awesome
and decisive power, seeking to insure that the open palm of imaginative rhetoric and poetry can flourish in a liberated nation.

        According to P. A. Duhamel and Merritt Y. Hughes, "Structurally
the Tenure of Kings and Magistrates may be considered one expanded
categorical syllogism," an extended proof of the proposition that tyrannical kings may lawfully be deposed and punished.[6] Although
Hughes maintains that the classical oratorical structure of the tract
is "constantly distorted by digressions replying to the main arguments" of the Presbyterians (PW, III:107), these replies are essential
to the logical and emotional structure. The first section (III:190-97)
aims blow after blow at those blocking the path to the freedom and
dignity which should have been renewed by tyrannicide. The initial
massive assault on the Presbyterians begets two additional and similar ones (III:192-94), the first of which I have used in the first chapter
to illustrate basic characteristics of Milton's prose. Then Milton
turns to another group of men incapable of exploiting the heroic political opportunities opened up by the execution of the king, men who are
not malicious, merely timid:

> Another sort there is, who comming in the cours of these affaires,
> to have thir share in great actions, above the form of Law or Cus-
> tom, at least to give thir voice and approbation, begin to swerve,
> and almost shiver at the Majesty and grandeur of som noble deed,
> as if they were newly enter'd into a great sin. [III:194]

But the relatively gentle treatment these men receive turns out to be
a digression, for Milton is soon firing off another thunderous blast at
the still unnamed Presbyterians: "Nor let any man be deluded . . .
onely surviving in thir own faction" (III:195-97). To introduce one's
argument with such major confrontations, each presented as a decisive
encounter, yet each apparently so indecisive as to require repetition,
is to proclaim both the urgency of the situation and the insecurity of
one's position and is to attempt, as in the divorce tracts, to alter the
shape of political reality by main force of rhetoric alone.
        The next section (III:197-212) consists of four closely argued ex-
positions of political theory, the first three of which I have analyzed
above. The gist of Milton's theory is stated towards the end of the
opening examination of the primal social contract:

> Then did they who now by tryal had found the danger and incon-
> veniences of committing arbitrary power to any, invent Laws

either fram'd, or consented to by all, that should confine and limit
the autority of whom they chose to govern them: that so man, of
whose failing they had proof, might no more rule over them, but
law and reason abstracted as much as might be from personal errors and frailties. [III:199-200]

As I have shown, the next two arguments seek to defend this achievement of political reason from encroaching absolutists, who would
override reason and law with lawless arbitrary power. The crucial
implication from the nature of rational constitutional government can
then be presented in its full logical clarity:

It follows lastly, that since the King or Magistrate holds his autoritie of the people, both originaly and naturally for their good
in the first place, and not his own, then may the people as oft as
they shall judge it for the best, either choose him or reject him,
retaine him or depose him though no Tyrant, meerly by the
liberty and right of free born Men, to be govern'd as seems to
them best. [III:206]

After defending this conclusion by scriptural exegesis, Milton establishes the point that follows directly from it, that if a free people may
depose any ruler, they may punish a tyrant. As a lawful king is a
great blessing to a free people, so a tyrant is a great "mischeife . . .
Against whom what the people lawfully may doe, as against a common
pest, and destroyer of mankinde, I suppose no man of cleare judgement
need goe furder to be guided then by the very principles of nature in
him" (III:212). A purely rational proof of Milton's case would have
ended here. "But because it is the vulgar folly of men to desert thir
own reason," because the establishment of political reason in England
is being attacked by the deformed and zealous arguments of the Presbyterians, Milton must proceed to a lengthy narration of the historical
evidence in favor of his position. This evidence is presented in more
or less chronological order, pagan testimony in favor of tyrannicide
rollowed by Jewish, early Christian, and medieval English examples
and statutes. The climax of the tract begins to come into view when
the historical survey arrives at the heroic resistance to tyrants on
the part of sixteenth-century Protestants: German, Dutch, and, above
all, Scotch Presbyterian.

The evidence thus flows smoothly into another battle with the English Presbyterians: "But what need these examples to Presbyterians,
I mean to those who now of late would seem so much to abhorr deposing, when as they to all Christendom have giv'n the latest and live-
liest example of doing it themselves" (III:227). If possible this battle
is waged on Milton's part even more sharply and furiously than it had
been in the introductory section. To "rise against the King and his

autority" defending anything unlawfully established is to renounce
"Supremacy and Allegeance" and depose such a king. That the Presbyterians have done exactly this is proved by "a seven years story
fresh in the memory of all men" (III:228). They have broken the
Oaths of Allegiance and Supremacy by defying the king's commands
and setting up the Parliament against him. As if this demonstration
were not sufficient, Milton repeats it in a more ruthlessly syllogistic
and sarcastic form:

> We know that King and Subject are relatives, and relatives have
> no longer being then in the relation; the relation between King
> and Subject can be no other then regal autority and subjection.
> Hence I inferr past their defending, that if the Subject who is one
> relative, take away the relation, of force he takes away also the
> other relative; but the Presbyterians who were one relative, that
> is to say Subjects, have for this sev'n years tak'n away the relation,
> that is to say the Kings autority, and thir subjection to it, ther-
> fore the Presbyterians for these sev'n years have remov'd and
> extinguished the other relative, that is to say the King, or to
> speak more in brief have depos'd him; not onely by depriving him
> the execution of his autoritie, but by conferring it upon others.
> [III:229–30]

The sarcasm derives from the repeated conjunction of the participants in a heroic drama (Presbyterians and king) with denatured ab-
stractions (relation and relative). By their base betrayal of the cause,
the Presbyterians have forced Milton to empty a major historical moment of its heroic content and frame it according to the arid formulas
of Scholastic discourse. The Presbyterians also began the process of
punishing and killing the king by making war on him, for by this action
they pronounced him an outlaw and rebel. Again a simple proof is
followed by a mordantly strict one:

> It must needs be clear to any man not avers from reason, that
> hostilitie and subjection are two direct and positive contraries;
> and can no more in one subject stand together in respect of the
> same King, then one person at the same time can be in two re-
> mote places. Against whom therfore the Subject is in act of
> hostility we may be confident that to him he is in no subjection:
> and in whom hostility takes place of subjection, for they can by
> no meanes consist together, to him the King can be not onely no
> King, but an enemie. [III:230]

The sarcastic tone of this demonstration, as though Milton were lec-
turing to a group of obtuse schoolboys, marks the beginning of a
steadily intensifying expression of polemical emotion, which builds

through the indignant rhetorical questions describing the Presbyterian role in the civil wars and through the discussion of their crafty insistence that a clause of allegiance to the king be inserted in the Solemn League and Covenant (III:231–33). Logic and emotion issue together at last into an overwhelming summary of the case against the Presbyterians:

> Thus having quite extinguisht all that could be in him of a King, and from a total privation clad him over, like another specifical thing, with formes and habitudes destructive to the former, they left in his person, dead as to Law, and all the civil right either of King or Subject, the life onely of a Prisner, a Captive and a Malefactor. Whom the equal and impartial hand of justice finding, was no more to spare then another ordinary man; not onely made obnoxious to the doom of Law by a charge more then once drawn up against him, and his own confession to the first Article at New- port, but summond and arraign'd in the sight of God and his people, curst & devoted to perdition worse then any Ahab, or Antiochus, with exhortation to curse all those in the name of God that made not Warr against him, as bitterly as Meroz was to be curs'd, that went not out against a Canaanitish King, almost in all the Sermons, Prayers, and Fulminations that have bin utter'd this sev'n yeares by those clov'n tongues of falsehood and dissention; who now, to the stirring up of new discord, acquitt him; and against thir own disciplin, which they boast to be the throne and scepter of Christ, absolve him, unconfound him, though unconverted, unrepentant, unsensible of all thir pretious Saints and Martyrs whose blood they have so oft laid upon his head: and now againe with a new sovran anointment can wash it all off, as if it were as vile, and no more to be reckon'd for, then the blood of so many Dogs in a time of Pestilence: giving the most opprobrious lye to all the acted zeale that for these many yeares hath filld thir bellies, and fed them fatt upon the foolish people. Ministers of sedition, not of the Gospel, who while they saw it manifestly tend to civil Warr and blood shed, never ceasd exasperating the people against him; and now that they see it likely to breed new commotion, cease not to incite others against the people that have sav'd them from him, as if sedition were thir onely aime, whether against him or for him. [III:234–36]

The first part of this excerpt ("Thus having . . . ordinary man") recapitulates the previous sarcastic logic. Then as Milton begins to describe how the king had already been brought to the bar before the formal trial, the logical case becomes an emotional one. There is an invisible transition between a description of the just proceedings

against the king and an indignant reaction to the greed and hypocrisy
of the Presbyterians, a transition that has been completed by the time
Milton adds the "Fulminations" of the Presbyterians to their sermons
and prayers. From this point on, the passage is conducted in the language and syntax of vehement abuse. The "Fulminations . . . have bin
utterd . . . by those clov'n tongues of falsehood and dissention," and
this phrase triggers a chain reaction of emotional explosions, which
is not exhausted until it has run through three loose and lengthy
clauses: a trailing relative pronoun clause ("who now . . ."), a participial extension of this ("giving the most opprobrious lye . . ."), and
an appositive reformulation of the same accusations ("Ministers of
sedition"). In this passage, it seems to me, Milton tries to draw together all the rhetorical energies of his treatise into one massively
decisive attack which would clear the Presbyterians out of the way
once and for all and make possible further imaginative recollection
of Truth by a liberated society.

By next turning from polemic to declare his confidence in the English people and to celebrate the just proceedings against the king,
Milton provides for the moment a rhetorical celebration of political
victory:

> And if the Parlament and Military Councel doe what they doe
> without precedent, if it appeare thir duty, it argues the more
> wisdom, vertue, and magnanimity, that they know themselves
> able to be a precedent to others. Who perhaps in future ages,
> if they prove not too degenerat, will look up with honour, and
> aspire toward these examplary, and matchless deeds of thir
> Ancestors, as to the highest top of thir civil glory and emula-
> tion. Which heretofore, in the persuance of fame and forren
> dominion, spent it self vain-gloriously abroad; but henceforth
> may learn a better fortitude, to dare execute highest Justice
> on them that shall by force of Armes endeavour the oppressing
> and bereaving of Religion and thir liberty at home: that no un-
> bridled Potentate or Tyrant, but to his sorrow for the future,
> may presume such high and irresponsible licence over man-
> kinde, to havock and turn upside-down whole Kingdoms of men,
> as though they were no more in respect of his perverse will
> then a Nation of Pismires. [III:237–38]

Here the army officers and parliamentary Independents Milton is
defending are borne aloft into a domain of pure and matchless political heroism. By resolutely defying the precedents of the corrupted
past, they have made it possible for the future to be a continuous
realization of truth in the structure of civil society. Were it not for

the perverse opposition of the Presbyterians this is the way Milton's
presentation of the historical evidence in favor of tyrannicide would
end: not in strenuous polemic, but in indulging the opportunity to
"soare a while as the Poets use" afforded him by the fact that his
final example of tyrannicide is the most heroic and significant one
in all human history. Unfortunately for the coherence of his idealistic rhetoric and politics, however, Milton finds it impossible to
surpass or even recreate the full imaginative vigor and resonance
he had achieved in Areopagitica. The imaginative consummation of
history is now a fact, not an expectation, but Milton seems unable to
build a coherent social vision upon it. Instead, he is still bothered
by the Presbyterians: "As for the party calld Presbyterian . . ."
(III:238). This phrase begins a calm exhortation of the members of
this party, entreating them to stand fast by the true principles which
have now become politically potent. But when Milton addresses the
Presbyterian leaders, "the Divines" (III:240), he is before long drawn
into another attempt to destroy their opposition by a new outburst of
amplificatory pyrotechnics. And still he cannot leave them alone,
confident that he has dealt their position a fatal blow. The evidence
from the writings of Luther, Calvin, and other impeccably orthodox
reformers appended at the end in the second edition constitutes a
kind of large-scale "trailing clause" in the structure of the tract,[7]
destroying all possibility of imaginative social vision in the round of
citation, argument, and enraged polemic which concludes the tract
(III:257–58).

Barker has accurately summarized the pattern of Milton's rhetorical career:

> The Areopagitica and Tetrachordon expressed Milton's most ex-
> treme interpretation of Christian liberty and its consequences.
> They were attacks on the repressive policy of the [Westminster]
> Assembly; and they were written while his confidence in the
> powers and destiny of the English people, led by God and sup-
> ported by his grace, was as yet scarcely diminished. Much of
> that confidence was carried over to his first political tracts;
> the execution of the King promised to begin the firm establish-
> ment of liberty. But the difficulties of the Commonwealth
> forced him to assume a defensive rather than offensive attitude;
> and his compositions between 1649 and 1660 reverse rather than
> reproduce the process by which the radicalism of 1645 had
> emerged from the reforming zeal of 1641.

In my opinion Barker is also correct to call the Tenure a work of
"confident enthusiasm" and to stress the millennial expectations that
were aroused anew in Milton by the trial and execution of the king.[8]

To this extent, the Tenure is an adaptation of the methods of Milton's most confident works, the divorce tracts and Areopagitica, to the fact that the millennium ushered in by tyrannicide was being perversely opposed by a powerful faction. But as I have argued, Milton is brought by his powerful logic and emotions to the verge of an imaginative celebration of a new age, only to find himself continuing to struggle with old enemies. The open-palmed rhetoric of Areopagitica could not achieve its perfected form on the wider stage of direct political advocacy, because on that wider stage such rhetoric encountered a configuration of political forces hostile to Milton's vision. Such rhetoric is replaced by repetitious applications of the logical and emotional closed fist that had been designed to aid in its fulfillment. Thus incorporated into the structure of the Tenure is a suggestion that the dangerous opposition of the Presbyterians can never be laid decisively to rest, and thus the Tenure stands stylistically as well as chronologically in the middle of the symmetrical pattern of Milton's rhetorical career outlined by Barker. Its poised logic and emotions seek to recreate the conditions for a more grandiose Areopagitica. Its trailing structure, endlessly proliferating these logical and pathetic proofs, whispers that this task probably cannot be performed. This structure betrays Milton's loss of faith in his expectation of the still time when there shall be no chiding and consequently inaugurates his later prose style, in which both idealism and polemic dismiss social reality as worthless.

"Eikonoklastes"

Eikonoklastes was published in October 1649 and reprinted in a slightly augmented version in 1650. In the brief outline that concludes my first chapter, I have focused on the significance of this tract's bibliographical history as contrasted with that of the widely popular Eikon Basilike. The sixty editions of the "Kings Book," not to mention the innumerable reprints of the prayers appended to each of its chapters, no doubt confirmed Milton's suspicion, latent in the structure of the Tenure, that his social ideals would never be realized. The great majority of Englishmen had evidently remained unmoved by political heroism and were persisting in their obtuse veneration of a crafty and effeminate tyrant (see above, p. 26).

The consequences of this perception for the tone of Milton's political prose were far-reaching. We can begin to understand them by examining some of the new material inserted into the second edition of the preface to Eikonoklastes. In the first edition Milton had been content to minimize the difficulty of his task: "I take it on me as a work assign'd rather, then by me chos'n or affected. Which was the cause both of beginning it so late, and finishing it so leasurely, in the

midst of other imployments and diversions" (III:339). In the second
edition, however, this confident statement cannot stand alone, since
by this time the people's folly and superstition have become manifest.
Here then is what is added to the quoted passage:

> And though well it might have seem'd in vaine to write at all;
> considering the envy and almost infinite prejudice likely to be
> stirr'd up among the Common sort, against what ever can be
> writt'n or gainsaid to the Kings book, so advantageous to a book
> it is, only to be a Kings, and though it be an irksom labour to
> write with industrie and judicious paines that which neither
> waigh'd, nor well read, shall be judg'd without industry or the
> paines of well judging, by faction and the easy literature of cus-
> tom and opinion, it shall be ventur'd yet, and the truth not
> smother'd, but sent abroad, in the native confidence of her single
> self, to earn, how she can, her entertainment in the world, and to
> finde out her own readers; few perhaps, but those few, such of
> value and substantial worth, as truth and wisdom, not respecting
> numbers and bigg names, have bin ever wont in all ages to be
> contented with. [III:339–40]

In the two subordinate clauses, each attempt to assert the principles
of truth is immediately borne down by a swarm of petty enemies.
Writing anything, "what ever can be writt'n or gainsaid to the Kings
book," stirs up at once "envy and almost infinite prejudice . . . among
the Common sort." To write with "industrie and judicious paines"
begets the opposite kind of superficial reading "by faction and the
easy literature of custom and opinion." But in the main clause Milton
makes the heroic gesture that surmounts all these obstacles: "it shall
be ventur'd yet . . . ." This fierce heroic energy is then sustained on
through the chain of amplifying clauses, reversing the situation that
prevailed in the subordinate clauses. The principles of truth keep
confronting and overcoming their own negations and reexpressing
themselves in more resounding, emphatic terms: "and the truth not
smother'd, but sent abroad, in the native confidence of her single self
. . . her own readers; few perhaps, but those few, such of value and
substantial worth . . . truth and wisdom, not respecting numbers and
bigg names, have bin ever wont in all ages to be contented with." Although Milton thus grandiosely portrays the reforming rhetorician as
a moral hero, steadfastly affirming the truth in a hostile world, he
explicitly denies that his grand gestures can have any effect on the
malignant configuration of political forces. His rhetoric will find its
fit audience though few, all those who do not need to be convinced. The
vast majority of the people, who will in a few years be clamoring for a
Restoration, remain under the sway of "faction and the easy literature
of custom and opinion" embodied in the king's false book.

In a sense, Milton is here recognizing not only political reality, but also the political limitations of his own rhetoric. If people will not hearken to ideals and eloquence, so much the worse for them and their politics. Hughes applies to Eikonoklastes a comment of Jonathan Richardson's on Paradise Lost: "a reader of Milton must be Always upon Duty; he is Surrounded with Sense, it rises in every Line, every Word is to the Purpose; There are no Lazy Intervals, All has been Consider'd, and Demands, and Merits Observation."[9] When such density of matter is unfolded with little support from emotional emphasis or imaginative coloring, we have a rhetorical persona disavowing rhetoric and politics, speaking in a tone of cold rational contempt for a nation that has neither eyes to see nor ears to hear the obvious truth. With a few significant exceptions to be discussed below, this is the prevailing tone of Eikonoklastes.

One aspect of this aloof and superior tone is to treat the king as a trivial opponent, easily and carelessly refuted. Charles had set himself up for this by claiming in his first sentence that "He call'd this last Parlament not more by others advice and the necessity of his affaires, then by his own chois and inclination" (III:350). Milton need only recall a history of royal disregard of Parliaments well-known to everyone:

> Till eight or nine years after, proceeding with a high hand in these enormities, and having the second time levied an injurious Warr against his native Countrie Scotland, and finding all those other shifts of raising Money, which bore out his first expedition, now to fail him, not of his own chois and inclination, as any Child may see, but urg'd by strong necessities, and the very pangs of State, which his own violent proceedings had brought him to, hee calls a Parlament; first in Ireland, which onely was to give him four Subsidies, and so to expire; then in England, where his first demand was but twelve Subsidies, to maintain a Scotch Warr, condemn'd and abominated by the whole Kingdom; promising thir greevances should be consider'd afterward. Which when the Parlament, who judg'd that Warr it self one of thir main greevances, made no hast to grant, not enduring the delay of his impatient will, or els fearing the conditions of thir grant, he breaks off the whole Session, and dismisses them and thir greevances with scorn and frustration. [III:353—54]

This turns Charles into a player-king, as fickle and heedless of true leadership as Richard II in the first half of Shakespeare's play. By the repeated participial constructions, he is made to move effortlessly along, "urg'd" by his own glib mistakes and foolish purposes

until he is forced to stop and do something rational: "hee calls a
Parlament." A Parliament should embody political reason by its
mere meeting and should produce it in its deliberations and decisions, but Charles empties this Parliament in advance of all possible rational meaning by the easy and superficial logic that compelled
him to call it into session. It therefore races along to an early dis-
solution: "which onely was to give him four Subsidies, and so to ex-
pire." As the king continues on his thoughtless and deceitful way
("promising thir greevances should be consider'd afterward"), the
English people and Parliament begin to embody the true rational
structure of the state: "a Scotch Warr, condemn'd and abominated
by the whole Kingdom . . . Which when the Parlament, who judg'd
that Warr it self one of thir main greevances, made no\hast to grant."
Representing the popular will and reason, Parliament tries to slow
down the lunatic pace of the king's activities, making "no hast" in
making policy more rationally. But the king plunges ahead, again
characterized by the smooth participial constructions: "not enduring
the delay of his impatient will, or els fearing the conditions of thir
grant, he breaks off the whole Session, and dismisses them and thir
greevances with scorn and frustration." The fluency of this narrative
demonstrates how easily bad political conduct perpetuates itself.
History becomes a facile surrender to trivial ambitions, running on
and on in a chronicle of unstructured, reasonless events. As regards
the speaker's tone of voice, the effect of this fluency is well summarized by a phrase near the middle of the passage, "as any Child may
see." To refute the king's inane book is no more than a boring exercise for a rational adult.

Occasionally, it is true, Milton speaks in a somewhat more committed manner, usually when he is claiming that the various events
of the Revolution had fulfilled his idealistic expectations. One such
event was the London "tumults" of 1642, provoked by the king's high-
handed treatment of Parliament. The king had charged that Parliament "hunt[ed] after Faction with their Hounds the Tumults:"

> And yet the Bishops could have told him, that Nimrod, the first
> that hunted after Faction is reputed, by ancient Tradition, the
> first that founded Monarchy; whence it appeares that to hunt
> after Faction is more properly the Kings Game; and those
> Hounds, which he calls the Vulgar, have bin oft'n hollow'd to
> from Court; of whom the mungrel sort have bin entic'd; the rest
> have not lost thir sent; but understood aright, that the Parlament
> had that part to act which he had fail'd in: that trust to discharge,
> which he had brok'n; that estate and honour to preserve, which
> was farr beyond his, the estate and honour of the Common-wealth,
> which he had imbezl'd. [III:466−67]

First Milton twists the king's glib image for use against him, giving it a rational symmetry ("the first that hunted after Faction . . . the first that founded Monarchy") and breaking it down for precise analysis ("and those Hounds, which he calls the Vulgar, have bit oft'n hollow'd to from Court; of whom the mungrel sort have bin entic'd"). When this analysis discovers the supporters of political reason and truth, "the rest" who "have not lost thir sent," the king's tasteless image is abandoned and replaced by a strong rational verb in order to do justice to these virtuous men who "but understood aright." In the parallelisms which flow from this gesture of political sanity, then, the sentence rises smoothly into a domain of pure reason, in which principled insights arise one after another to balance and counteract the king's willful irrationality: "but understood aright, that the Parlament had that part to act which he had fail'd in; that trust to discharge, which he had brok'n; that estate and honour to preserve, which was farr beyond his, the estate and honour of the Common-wealth, which he had imbezl'd." However, the tidy way in which the more leisurely rhythm of the final parallel member rounds the passage off, and indeed the very exactitude of the passage's formal balance, both generate an effect explored in detail in my interpretation of The Readie and Easie Way. The construction suggests that this portrayal of a purely and fully rational populace is unreal, a wish-fulfilling attempt to precipitate something of value from the tumult and shouting.

I do not mean that Milton is deceiving himself here, but rather that in this tract he is beginning to pretend ironically and disdainfully that the institution of rational ideals in English society has been as "readie and easie" as his own polemical victories over the king. I have found only one passage in Eikonoklastes in which Milton seems to have convinced himself that the resistance to the king did indeed represent political heroism, the passage defending Parliament's role in the first civil war:

> For if neither God nor nature put civil power in the hands of any whomsoever, but to a lawfull end, and commands our obedience to the autority of Law onely, not to the Tyrannical force of any person, and if the Laws of our Land have plac'd the Sword in no man's single hand, so much as to unsheath against a forren enemie, much less upon the native people, but have plac't it in that elective body of the Parlament, to whom the making, repealing, judging, and interpreting of Law it self was also committed, as was fittest, so long as wee intended to bee a free Nation, and not the Slaves of one mans will, then was the King himself disobedient and rebellious to that Law by which he raign'd; and by autority of Parlament to raise armes against him in defence of Law and

Libertie, we doe not onely think, but beleeve and know was justi-
fiable both by the Word of God, the Laws of the Land, and all lawfull Oaths; and they who sided with him fought against all these.
[III:529]

This is the more energetic and strenuous utterance of Milton's previous tracts, painstakingly elevating Parliament's armed resistance to
the king into the rational order of the universe. Quite apart from the
fact that Milton's sweeping interpretation of the "Laws of our Land"
is wide open to the many legal disputes which were one of the major
sources of the conflict, there are many purely theoretical difficulties
concealed in the massive assurance of this intricate and ample decla-
mation. Milton simply assumes that the people in their elections, and
the Parliament in its "making, repealing, judging, and interpreting of
Law it self," will always have a "lawfull end" in view, ignoring the
possibility of oligarchy or tyranny imposed by the majority. As
Hobbes was first to point out, these conceptual problems became
glaringly prominent in the Defensio Secunda, in which Milton was
forced to defend the oligarchies of the Commonwealth and Protectorate in order to avoid the majority's tyranny of Restoration.[10] Nevertheless, the passage succeeds in transforming tautology into an image
of political grandeur by incorporating the particular disputes of the
1640s into what purports to be a structure of universally valid logic
and principle. In ruling by "Tyrannical force" and in making war on
his people, the king has been disobedient to everything, the laws of the
land and the Law of God and Nature of which these are a reflection.
He has thus defined himself as a rebel.[11] If the people intend to continue to define themselves by liberty, obedience to such a ruler is
logically impossible. The people are in the strictest sense commanded by their own rational dignity to resist him. The sentence enforces this sense of glorious necessity by issuing smoothly into its
tautological conclusions, in which the king's own words are swept into
the tide of freedom: "then was . . . he raign'd; and by autority . . .
Lawful Oaths . . . ."

But Milton's awareness that the task assigned him cannot be performed, or his lack of interest in performing it, becomes clear when
he defends the trial and execution of the king. The anecdote from
Josephus and the Apocrypha soon develops into an allegory of Truth
and Justice, similar to the set-piece panegyrics on Discipline and
Zeal in The Reason of Church Government and the Apology.[12] The
foundations are thus laid for a passionate and imaginative celebration of tyrannicide which would be built on the arguments developed
in the Tenure and applied throughout this tract. Significantly, however, Milton does not proceed in this manner; he never coherently

applies the allegory to the specific events of 1649. Instead, he trails
off into a rather forlorn expression of the wish that such a rhetoric
were possible:

> And if by sentence thus writt'n it were my happiness to set free
> the minds of English men from longing to returne poorly under
> that Captivity of Kings, from which the strength and supreme
> Sword of Justice hath deliverd them, I shall have don a work not
> much inferior to that of Zorobabel: . . . Which I shall yet not
> despaire to doe, if they in this Land whose minds are yet Captive,
> be but as ingenuous to acknowledge the strength and supremacie
> of Justice, as that heathen king was, to confess the strength of
> truth: . . . But if a King may doe among men whatsoever is his
> will and pleasure, and notwithstanding be unaccountable to men,
> then contrary to this magnifi'd wisdom of Zorobabel, neither
> Truth nor Justice, but the King is strongest of all other things.
> [III:585]

This is followed, not by any real attempt to take on the strenuous
rhetorical task of setting free "the minds of English men from longing
to returne poorly under that Captivity of Kings," which for Milton
would mean exhorting the people to live up to the social vision which
tyrannicide has made possible, but rather by more of the "readie and
easie" rational argument which has prevailed throughout the tract.[13]

Despite the disavowal of despair in the passage just quoted, the
corollary to the aloof argumentation of Eikonoklastes is the vehement
polemic we have seen in the Tenure, the divorce tracts, and the antiprelatical tracts. If the people will not attend to lucid demonstrations
of truth, they are to be condemned as sharply as the Presbyterians
had been. These passages of denunciation are admissions of rhetorical defeat, testifying to the reformer's inability continuously to sustain his cold rational poise in a world that has replaced reason with
superstition. Milton says in the preface that the people's failure to
consummate the revolution is the result of their long exposure to the
corrupt precepts of the bishops and to the more recent perfidious
behavior of the Presbyterians.[14] But this temperate explanation is
largely forgotten by the time we reach the unequivocal and outraged
expressions against the people's base servility that erupt so promi-
nently in the last two chapters. As we might expect, these passages
were expanded and intensified in the second edition, for by the time
of its publication it must have seemed to Milton no longer possible to
explain away the people's enthusiastic approval of the Eikon as anything other than evidence of their complete unworthiness. The most
abusive of these passages is significantly placed at the very end of the
tract:

> Such Prayers as these may happly catch the People, as was in-
> tended: but how they please God, is to be much doubted, though
> pray'd in secret, much less writt'n to be divulg'd. Which perhaps
> may gaine him after death a short, contemptible, and soon fading
> reward; not what he aims at, to stirr the constancie and solid
> firmness of any wise Man, or to unsettle the conscience of any
> knowing Christian, if he could ever aime at a thing so hopeless,
> and above the genius of his Cleric elocution, but to catch the
> worthles approbation of an inconstant, irrational, and Image-
> doting rabble; that like a credulous and hapless herd, begott'n
> to servility, and inchanted with these popular institutes of Tyran-
> ny, subscrib'd with a new device of the Kings Picture at his
> praiers, hold out both thir eares with such delight and ravish-
> ment to be stigmatiz'd and board through in witness of thir own
> voluntary and beloved baseness. [III:601][15]

Milton acknowledges the potency of the king's rhetoric even as he
seeks to deny it. He first tries to dismiss the king's stratagems in
a curt, decisive phrase ("a short, contemptible, and soon fading reward") and to defend against them with his fit audience though few
("the constancie and solid firmness of any wise Man, . . . the conscience of any knowing Christian"). But in the second half of the long
antithesis ("not what . . . but . . ."), the king's "reward" instead of
fading grows ever more certain. The earlier phrase of dismissal,
"a short, contemptible, and soon fading reward," is replaced by the
parallel cadence of "an inconstant, irrational, and Image-doting
rabble." This is what the king has posthumously mobilized, and the
further denunciations attached in the second edition do not make the
rabble any less dangerous. On the contrary, they expand on the
numbers and strength of these unregenerate masses: "that like . . .
begott'n . . . inchanted . . . subscrib'd." As is usual in Miltonic sentences of this type, emotional energy is stored up and concentrated
in the suspended participial clauses, then exploded into the resolving
predication, but this time the resolution is into lucid desolation: "hold
out both thir eares with such delight and ravishment to be stigmatiz'd
and board through in witness of thir own voluntary and beloved base-
ness." The anger of this passage is the last frustrated twist of Milton's political hopes, but its open-endedness represents his dawning
recognition of political futility and thus means the same thing as the
disdainful tone of the coolly poised sections. Indeed Milton proceeds
to end the tract with this other mode of political withdrawal, taking
refuge in the fit audience though few: "The rest, whom perhaps ignorance without malice, or some error, less then fatal, hath for the time
misledd, on this side Sorcery or obduration, may find the grace and
good guidance to bethink themselves, and recover" (III:601).

As Sirluck has pointed out, because of the need to refute the king's potent lies and errors one by one, Eikonoklastes has no "independent" rhetorical structure.[16] But the contrasting tonal elements I have analyzed will become sources of a new kind of antirhetorical structure at the close of Milton's political career ten years later. What begins to emerge in this tract and will then be systematically developed is a form of prose discourse that insists upon the gap between idealism and the ferocious polemic of the antiprelatical tracts. Idealism now acknowledges that it cannot dignify social reality by its imaginative rhetoric, but this recognition produces not a more "realistic" or plain style, but radical proposals argued as though readers and political contexts did not exist, on the one hand, and polemics which suggest the catastrophic momentum of unregenerate events, on the other.

THE TRACTS OF 1659–1660

During the nine years that intervened between the second edition of Eikonoklastes and the Treatise of Civil Power, Milton's prose career came to what he himself considered to be a noble and heroic climax in his Latin Defences of the English People. Even the second of these, however, fails to recapture the unique imaginative eloquence of Areopagitica, and this, I believe, is directly attributable to Milton's loss of faith in the Populus Anglicus he claimed to be defending. It has been the premise of this study that Milton's prose rhetoric could generate a dimension of imaginative appeal only when Milton "digressed" from social reality or when he could believe that the people were beginning to live by the stern but exhilarating dictates of Christian liberty. In Areopagitica he professed to believe this, which is the major reason the oration is his one fully coherent and imaginative and optimistic prose work. The Tenure struggles to sustain this faith, never mentioning the execution of the king except in a context of highly abstracted notions of heroic justice, and Eikonoklastes contains Milton's first clear responses to a sense of lost illusions. The people had defected from a potential Christian humanist revolution in the very hour of liberation, and any lingering traces of political optimism Milton may still have entertained must have been swept aside by the people's failure to support the Commonwealth and Protectorate.[1]

This most notable political fact of the 1650s made irrevocable the divorce between ideals and social reality which had always been implicit in Milton's rhetoric. Milton simply pretends that the various kingless governments which came and went between 1649 and 1660 perfectly embody his standards of right reason and heroic virtue.[2] Thus his commitment in the Defences to Cromwell and his clique (although this commitment is qualified by the praise of John Bradshaw), and thus his reply to De Moulin's telling insistence on the narrow oligarchical basis of the Commonwealth's power:

> Whence I insist that [the Independents] were also superior both in law and in merit, for nothing is more natural, nothing more just, nothing more useful or more advantageous to the human race than that the lesser obey the greater, not the lesser number the greater number, but the lesser virtue the greater virtue, the lesser wisdom the greater wisdom. Them whose power lies in wisdom, experience, industry, and virtue will, in my opinion, however small

their number, be a majority and prove more powerful in balloting everywhere than any mere number, however great. [IV:636]

Whatever the accuracy of this assessment of the Independents, Du Moulin was correct in insisting that their regime depended on the "military excellence" of Cromwell, not on superior wisdom, virtue, and piety. Cromwell's death in September 1658 brought on a futile search for a legitimate civil authority, but Cromwell's army remained the most potent force in England, deposing and installing legislative assemblies and magistrates as it saw fit. These chaotic circumstances insured that Milton's idealistic proposals became (in his last pamphlets) ironic pretenses: proposals made first to Richard Cromwell's short-lived Parliament, then to the reinstated Rump, and finally and most disdainfully of all, to the royalist Long Parliament.[3] All of these were utterly powerless creatures of the army, but Milton speaks to each one as though it were reason and virtue incarnate, a body of heroic men who would heed his poised rational advice.

"A Treatise of Civil Power" and
"Means to Remove Hirelings"

The Treatise was published in February 1659, shortly after Richard's Parliament began its futile deliberations on 27 January. Its companion piece, Hirelings, appeared six months later, after the Rump had become the ostensible civil authority. Parker believes that in these two works Milton made public "some of the least shocking conclusions" of De Doctrina Christiana.[4] They may not be shocking, but the views here set forth are certainly as radical as Milton's positions usually are, amounting to no less than an argument for the withering away of the church. The style in which they are urged has been aptly described by Barbara Lewalski as being "unusual among Milton's pamphlets for its brevity and succinctness, its emotional restraint, its plain and unadorned diction, and its comparatively straightforward syntax."[5] I would claim that these features, particularly "emotional restraint," constitute a rhetoric which makes no concessions or overtures to the reader. The opening words of the Treatise set the tone for both tracts: "Two things there be which have bin ever found working much mischief to the church of God, and the advancement of truth; force on the one side restraining, and hire on the other side corrupting the teachers thereof. Few ages have bin since the ascension of our Saviour, wherin the one of these two, or both together have not prevaild" (CM, VI:4). Milton begins his political career and his first tract, Of Reformation, by encompassing the besetting sins and errors in church history within a massive structure of passionate utterance. These final works simply and briefly set down the settled conclusions of a meditation upon it, analyzing

ecclesiastical corruptions rather than seeking to wipe them out by
sheer force of speech: "Two things there be . . . force on the one
side . . . and hire on the other . . . the one of these two, or both together." To write with such precision and poise is to pretend that
one is operating in a world prepared to govern itself by the dictates
of pure and detached reason. In the passage from Of Reformation,
a committed believer struggles to make all ecclesiastical experience
conform to his idealistic sensibility. Here a disembodied mind neatly
encloses an intellectual problem.

The tracts are so serenely and effortlessly rational that a central
point of the Treatise can be proved by a few well-chosen words:

> First it cannot be deni'd, being the main foundation of our protes-
> tant religion, that we of these ages, having no other divine rule or
> autoritie from without us warrantable to one another as a com-
> mon ground but the holy scripture, and no other within us but the
> illumination of the Holy Spirit so interpreting that scripture as
> warrantable only to our selves and to such whose consciences
> we can so perswade, can have no other ground in matters of
> religion but only from the scriptures. And these being not pos-
> sible to be understood without this divine illumination, which no
> man can know at all times to be in himself, much less to be at
> any time for certain in any other, it follows cleerly, that no man
> or body of men in these times can be the infallible judges or
> determiners in matters of religion to any other mens consciences
> but thir own. [CM, VI:6]

The tone of the passage emerges from its participial constructions,
"being the main foundation," "having no other divine rule," and "these
being not possible to be understood." These bestow upon the argument an aura of a priori purity. The speaker is doing what any rational man expounding these questions would do, gathering together
what is securely known in order to determine what is to be done,
unfolding the innate implications of the terms of debate everyone
accepts, in this case the pure meaning of the term "protestant." The
conclusion that all human authorities in religion are illegitimate
"follows cleerly" once the reader has assented to those assured
participials. Of course the fact that the obvious needs to be belabored
at all suggests that such readers are scarce in 1659. If they were not,
there would be no debate and no pamphlets from the pen of Milton; all
social institutions, including the church, would be as superbly rational as this mode of discourse.

What the social landscape of England would become were its citi-
zens guided by right reason is suggested more fully in Hirelings.

Milton answers one of the objections to abolishing tithes by proposing to renew the Apostolic tradition:

> I answer, that if they stay there a year or two, which was the longest time usually staid by the apostles in one place, it may suffice to teach them, who will attend and learn, all the points of religion necessary to salvation; then sorting them into several congregations of a moderat number, out of the ablest and zealousest among them to create elders, who, exercising and requiring from themselves what they have learnd (for no learning is retaind without constant exercise and methodical repetition) may teach and govern the rest: and so exhorted to continue faithful and stedfast, they may securely be committed to the providence of God and the guidance of his holy spirit, till God may offer som opportunitie to visit them again and to confirme them: which when they have don, they have don as much as the apoltles were wont to do in propagating the gospel. [CM, VI: 77–78]

Each of these clauses proceeds from a potent gesture of creation, making the poorest of English villages into a place of continuous and vital rational communication: "to teach them, who will attend and learn, . . . out of the ablest and zealousest among them to create elders, who, exercising and requiring from themselves what they have learnd . . . may teach and govern the rest." This interdependent religious virility among apostles, ministers, and people soon draws into the community the most vital and essential presence of all: "they may securely be committed to the providence of God and the guidance of his holy spirit, till God may offer som opportunitie to visit them again and to confirme them." The smooth transitions between the stages of this creative process ("then sorting . . . who, exercising . . . and so exhorted . . . which when they have don") signify the effortless organic quality of a reformation that relies on God's ordained procedures of rational exhortation.

To the subsequent hirelings' objection that richer churches could not afford to subsidize the religious life of poor villages, Milton replies that itinerant ministers could if necessary be paid out of public revenues:

> And those uses may be, no doubt, much rather then as glebes and augmentations are now bestowd, to grant such requests as these of the churches; or to erect in greater number all over the land schooles and competent libraries to those schooles, where languages and arts may be taught free together, without the needles, unprofitable and inconvenient removing to another place. So all the land would be soone better civiliz'd, and they who are taught

freely at the publick cost, might have thir education given them
on this condition, that therewith content, they should not gadd for
preferment out of thir own countrey, but continue there thankful
for what they receivd freely, bestowing it as freely on thir countrey, without soaring above the meannes wherin they were born.
[CM, VI:79–80]

The impact of this passage is similar to that of the preceding one. A
gesture of creation begets the institutions of rational freedom: "to
erect in greater number all over the land schooles and competent
libraries to those schooles." Besides the external benefits of universal instruction and the saving of time, trouble, and money, these
schools would amend the national life. But the way in which the passage moves so readily and easily to its vistas of social regeneration
("So all the land . . .") has the same effect as the offhanded manner
in which Milton advises the English clergy to emulate the Apostles
in the passage above; neither proposal is meant as a serious practical proposition in the England of 1659. Each is addressed to an
imaginary audience of purely rational and principled Christian citi-
zens who do not need Milton's counsels, and each expresses a corresponding contempt for the actual balance of social forces.

Cool superiority to the realities of the situation occasionally yields
to polemical attacks on it, although these are here more subdued than
they were in Eikonoklastes and both more subdued and less frequent
than they will be in The Readie and Easie Way. In the Treatise, Milton answers as follows the objection that toleration would make
church discipline impossible:

Let who so will interpret or determin, so it be according to true
church-discipline; which is exercis'd on them only who have will-
ingly joind themselves in that covnant of union, and proceeds only
to a separation from the rest, proceeds never to any corporal in-
forcement or forfeture of monie; which in spiritual things are the
two arms of Anti-christ, not of the true church; the one being an
inquisition, the other no more then a temporal indulgence of sin
for monie, whether by the church exacted or by the magistrate;
both the one and the other a temporal satisfaction for what Christ
hath satisfied eternally; a popish commuting of penaltie, corporal
for spiritual; a satisfaction to man especially to the magistrate,
for what and to whom we owe none. [CM, VI:9–10]

That the second part of the passage, after "forfeture of monie," was
written at all is a sign that the posture of detached exposition has
been disguising social realities. From a perspective of reason and
principle, the case is made in the first part. It is weakened, I believe deliberately, by dwelling on degradations of spirit into flesh,

especially towards the end when analytical rebuttal ("the two arms
. . . the one being . . . the other no more . . .") gives way to repetitious appositions. As in the abusive passage just prior to the end of
Eikonoklastes, to finish off vehemently a discussion which begins
calmly is to insinuate that corruption persists and will reemerge
despite one's best rational efforts.

Such intimations of failure are kept to a minimum in both tracts,
however, and the pretense of a poised expositor of first principles
reasoning with men capable of responding on this level is maintained
by and large throughout. The most useful analogue to these two little
pamphlets is Paradise Regained. The spare, frugal style of the brief
epic amounts to poetry as challenge but not as invitation.[6] The corresponding prose style here renounces rhetoric except as a subtle
and ironically scornful challenge to a nation inconsiderate of principles lucidly expounded. Near the end of twenty years of strenuous
public advocacy, Milton suggests that a concentration of expository
energies on essential principles should function the way the outward
weakness and inner strength of true religion does, that it should suffice to overcome all the tomes and tirades of this world. If it will
not, as appears all but certain, the uncompromising idealist is justified by considerations which transcend politics: "If I be not heard
nor beleevd, the event will bear me witnes to have spoken truth: and
I in the mean while have borne my witnes not out of season to the
church and to my countrey" (CM, VI:100).

"The Readie and Easie Way to
Establish a Free Commonwealth"

The publication dates of The Readie and Easie Way are more significant for the analyst of Milton's rhetoric than are those of any
other of Milton's pamphlets. The first edition was probably largely
finished before 21 February 1660 and published between 21 February
and 3 March. The Restoration had become inevitable on 21 February
when General Monck, who had brought his army with him from Edin-
burgh to London, forced the Rump to readmit those members of the
Long Parliament who had been secluded by Pride's Purge in 1648 because of their opposition to the proceedings against Charles I. These
mostly Presbyterian secluded members were well known to be royalists.[7] Milton casually refers to these events in the first paragraph
of the first edition: "(the Parlament now sitting more full and frequent)." The second edition appeared shortly before the Restoration,
in late April 1660, Milton having extensively rewritten his pamphlet
in response to the writs for electing a new Parliament which the Long
Parliament had approved on 16 March.[8] As he had done in the De-

fences and, most recently, in the two antiecclesiastical pamphlets of
1659, Milton continues to address those in power as if they were reason and virtue incarnate, capable of giving a fair and respectful hear-
ing to his republican arguments. But this publication history, with
Milton twice revising his pamphlet to bring it up to date, indicates
quite clearly that this prose style of uncompromising right reason
has become consciously disingenuous, a gesture of disdain for the
obvious balance of political forces. Otherwise we must suppose that
Milton, while aware of the activities of General Monck and the Long
Parliament, somehow managed to be the only man in England inno-
cent of their implications. He thus pretends that the Long Parliament's "sitting more full and frequent" will increase his chances of
persuading it, although he well knew that this very fact virtually
guaranteed the Restoration.[9] Likewise in the second edition, as we
shall see, Milton discusses the Parliament about to be elected with a
cool disregard of the crucial fact that it was certain to restore a
Stuart king.

What we have learned about the effect of the Revolution's imminent
failure on Milton's later prose style puts us in a position to assess
the degree of utopianism in his final political proposals. Zera S.
Fink has shown that the theory of the mixed state was one of the
"chief bases of seventeenth-century utopianism." Harrington and
others believed a mixed state could be constituted so as to be a "perfectly balanced government, in which the defects of fallen man would
be so compensated for that it would last unimpaired and unchanged
forever." After tracing the development of Milton's ideas on the
mixed state through all his prose works, Fink argues that in the final
version of them in The Readie and Easie Way, Milton projected an
eternally enduring government. This plan was utopian, but uncon-
sciously so, because Milton hoped for its actual adoption.[10] Barbara
Lewalski, denying any utopian implications, emphasizes the rhetorical pragmatism of The Readie and Easie Way. Milton did try to get
his plan adopted. One point she does not make is that the outline of
the proposed government, a legislative body and an executive council
some of the members of which are to be chosen from the legislature,
is clearly derived from Milton's years of membership on the Council
of State, many of the members of which were also members of the
various Parliaments that came and went between 1649 and 1660. She
discusses the changes Milton made for the second edition, by which
he sought to attract Harringtonians, Fifth Monarchists, and even
Presbyterians into an antiroyalist coalition.[11] But as I have argued,
even Milton must have realized that such maneuvers would prove futile by April 1660. The apparent realism Lewalski discerns derives,
I believe, from a premise that is now willfully and ironically utopian,

the premise, namely, that he is addressing a nation still open to the
pure reason of a republican. This rational, and therefore utopian,
pragmatism is perhaps most clearly evident in a passage from <u>A
Letter to a Friend</u>, written in late 1659, between the Rump's two brief
terms in office:

> Being now in Anarchy, without a counselling and governing Power;
> and the Army, I suppose, finding themselves insufficient to dis-
> charge at once both Military and Civil Affairs, the first thing to
> be found out with all speed, without which no Commonwealth can
> subsist, must be a Senate, or General Council of State, in whom
> must be the Power, first, to preserve the publick Peace, next the
> Commerce with Foreign Nations; and lastly, to raise Monies for
> the Management of these Affairs: this must either be the Parlia-
> ment readmitted to sit, or a Council of State allow'd of by the
> Army, since they only now have the Power. The Terms to be
> stood on are, Liberty of Conscience to all professing Scripture to
> be the Rule of thir Faith and Worship; and the Abjuration of a
> single Person. [CM, VI:104]

<u>The Readie and Easie Way</u> is a confrontation between this kind of suc-
cinct unadorned reasoning and what constantly interrupts it or modi-
fies it, polemics against recalcitrant political circumstances,
conducted in a style which conveys a recognition of the imminent and
inevitable defeat of the Good Old Cause.[12]

E. N. S. Thompson says that the syntax of <u>The Readie and Easie
Way</u> is for the most part coordinate. The long sentences are not constructed; they are simply strung together.[13] Here, for example, is a
typically dense and extended characterization of monarchy:

> Wheras a king must be ador'd like a Demigod, with a dissolute
> and haughtie court about him, of vast expence and luxurie, masks
> and revels, to the debaushing of our prime gentry both male and
> female; not in their passetimes only, but in earnest, by the loos
> imploiments of court service, which will be then thought honor-
> able. There will be a queen also of no less charge; in most like-
> lihood outlandish and a Papist; besides a queen mother such
> alreadie; together with both thir courts and numerous train: then
> a royal issue, and ere long severally thir sumptuous courts; to
> the multiplying of a servile crew, not of servants only, but of no-
> bility and gentry, bred up then to the hopes not of public, but of
> court offices; to be stewards, chamberlains, ushers, grooms,
> even of the close-stool; the lower thir mindes debas'd with court
> opinions, contrarie to all vertue and reformation, the haughtier
> will be thir pride and profuseness. [CM, VI:120]

Milton here fully acknowledges what we saw him beginning to admit
in Eikonoklastes and the antiecclesiastical pamphlets, the accumu-
lating force of the flawed political circumstances his rhetoric had
always sought to confront and transform. A subordinated syntax
shaping an abundance of content attempts to encompass and, in a
sense, defeat as many opponents and hostile circumstances as possible. But a linear polemic such as this one suggests an infinite
proliferation of corrupted social conditions which cannot all be
transformed. As soon as one is condemned and disposed of, the
republican voice must encounter another and another and another.
The connecting links of the passage enhance this effect: "not in their
passetimes only, but in earnest, . . . a queen also . . . besides a queen
mother such alreadie; together with both thir courts . . . then a royal
issue, and ere long severally . . . to the multiplying of a servile crew,
not of servants only, but of nobility and gentry, bred up then to the
hopes not of public, but of court offices; to be stewards . . . even of
the close-stool" (my emphasis). These transitions generate an em-
barrassment of riches, a feeling that the reformer has been presented with more raw material than he can ultimately cope with.
They also generate a sense of the dizzy momentum of events: the
advent of Charles II will lead English society straight to the close-
stool. Warfaring rhetoric has turned into a wayfaring which can only
conclude with a lucid perception that the Restoration will result in
the flat contradiction of all true ideals:[14] "the lower thir minds de-
bas'd with court opinions, contrarie to all vertue and reformation, the
haughtier will be thir pride and profuseness."

My point, then, is that in this tract Milton completes the alteration of his prose style which he had begun in Eikonoklastes. It now
thoroughly and consciously reflects a political situation controlled
by Milton's opponents. Traveling openly through a hostile social
landscape, denouncing what cannot be reformed, represents the only
self-respecting posture still available to a virtuous citizen. All
others may plunge ahead to the closestool, but the genuine republican
will move firmly along his own path, dramatizing the process he witnesses all around him and stating clearly what it means. This syntax
and this posture prevail throughout this section of the pamphlet, although the sense of being surrounded by hostile and irresistibly powerful forces emerges most often in passages attacking the nation at
large for its counterrevolutionary backsliding. One such passage
more or less concludes this particular stretch of polemic:

> That a nation should be so valorous and courageous to winn thir
> liberty in the field, and when they have wonn it, should be so
> heartless and unwise in thir counsels, as not to know how to use

> it, value it, what to do with it or with themselves; but after ten or
> twelve years prosperous warr and contestation with tyrannie,
> basely and besottedly to run their necks again into the yoke which
> they have broken, and prostrate all the fruits of thir victorie for
> naught at the feet of the vanquishd, besides our loss of glorie,
> and such an example as kings or tyrants never yet had the like to
> boast of, will be an ignominie if it befall us, that never yet befell
> any nation possessd of thir libertie; worthie indeed themselves,
> whatsoever they be, to be for ever slaves: but that part of the
> nation which consents not with them, as I perswade me of a great
> number, far worthier then by their means to be brought into the
> same bondage. [CM, VI:123]

In this sentence Milton appears to be writing as he does in his earlier
prose. He confronts the forces that threaten his cause, broadening
the issues and the focus of his indignation through a series of subordinate and interpolated clauses, then explosively releases the accumulated emotional and conceptual energies in the long-delayed
predication, "will be an ignominie if it befall us, that never yet befell
and nation possessd of thir libertie." The people are conclusively
indicted by this procedure. Their errors and failings are seen to
exist, quite literally, within a larger order, within an elaborately
constructed and massive edifice of principled judgment. But Milton
will not allow himself or anyone else to pretend that the enemies of
reformation and revolution can be so thoroughly crushed in the
spring of 1660. This is suggested by the way in which the climactic
thrust of the major predication is dissipated by a series of antidemo-
cratic afterthoughts: "worthie indeed themselves, whatsoever they
be, to be for ever slaves: but that part of the nation which consents
not with them, as I perswade me of a great number, far worthier then
by their means to be brought into the same bondage." Coordinate or
trailing members appended to such a carefully and elaborately subordinated period as this one demonstrate Milton's recognition that he
is as unable to deal conclusively with the masses of sentimental
royalists as he is with the disastrous logic of events or the densely
trivial society a Restoration will produce.
    If the situation is governed, so to speak, by irrationality, per-
versity, and madness, then the rational way can only be made to appear ready and easy by coolly ignoring the actual situation while
making one's proposals. This Milton proceeds to do in the section
immediately following.[15] His first detailed presentation of his plan
is a more elaborate version of the passage from A Letter to a Friend
quoted above:

> For the ground and basis of every just and free government

(since men have smarted so oft for commiting all to one person)
is a general council of ablest men, chosen by the people to con-
sult of public affairs from time to time for the common good. In
this Grand Councel must the sovrantie, not transferrd, but delegated only, and as it were deposited, reside; with this caution
they must have the forces by sea and land committed to them for
preservation of the common peace and libertie; must raise and
manage the public revenue, at least with som inspectors deputed
for satisfaction of the people, how it is imploid; must make or
propose, as more expressly shall be said anon, civil laws; treat
of commerce, peace, or warr with forein nations, and for the
carrying on som particular affairs with more secrecie and ex-
pedition, must elect, as they have alreadie out of thir own number and others, a Councel of State. [CM, VI:125–26]

Milton leads up to this outline by suggesting with superbly ironic
naivete that the writs which had been proclaimed on 16 March for the
election of a "free" (i.e., other than the Long) Parliament could serve
as the basis for implementing his plan. The new Parliament could
simply constitute itself as his perpetual senate. Milton knew perfectly well how the elections would turn out. The new Parliament would
be dominated by Cavaliers and Presbyterians and would proceed immediately to bring in the son of Charles I. Disdaining these certain-
ties, Milton imagines the way history would go if men were the least
bit reasonable. As he presents it here, that way is certainly ready
and easy, for he blandly forgets the hostile and irresistible forces
he has just embodied so compellingly in the preceding section. Despite its dominance elsewhere, he simply alludes to the danger of a
restoration in a decorous parenthesis, in the midst of an exposition
of first principles. He minutely defines the constitutional status of
the "Grand Councel" ("the sovrantie, not transferrd, but delegated
only, and as it were deposited") and thus provides a rational solution
for one of the primary causes of the tumult and conflict of the previous twenty years. The inverted formal syntax of this discussion of
sovereignty initiates a series of parallel clauses, firmly securing
the necessary functions of government in good order: "must . . .
reside . . . they must have . . . must raise . . . must make or propose . . . treat . . . must elect." The passage has all the balance and
poise of a paragraph by Burke, but it eschews the characteristically
warm emotional appeal of Burke's prose. It projects a state divorced
from tradition and existing social structures, founded instead on pure
reason. The implication is that only by extracting from its political
life all given emotional commitments could England retain in 1660
even the remotest hope that emotion would someday become socially

creative rather than disastrous: "for it may be referrd to time, so we be still going on by degrees to perfection" (CM, VI:132).

Milton embodies the impossibility of this hope for a ready and easy rational way, at least for the foreseeable future, in the organization of the pamphlet, which alternates from beginning to end between sections conveying a sense that events have passed quite beyond republican or rational governance and sections explaining the futile but reasonable plan for stabilizing the Revolution. A description of the rational state is superseded by a denunciation of the irrational realities of the political situation, is restated more copiously and fully, and is again superseded. Near the beginning, Milton makes explicit the recognition of political reality enacted throughout in the style and structure: "If thir absolute determination be to enthrall us, before so long a Lent of Servitude, they may permitt us a little Shroving-time first, wherin to speak freely, and take our leaves of Libertie" (CM, VI:111). He then proceeds to a calm recapitulation of English history since 1641 (CM, VI:112ff.), arguing that the actions of Parliament during the 1640s were eminently rational, grounded as they were in the Law of Nature. Milton is here attempting to depict a political situation fully governed by general principles, but when he comes to the period of negotiations with Charles I in 1647–48, the shape and rhythm of his discourse become less poised and steady, more tangled and difficult, reflecting the nearly unmanageable crisis which developed at that time:

> And yet they were not to learn that a greater number might be corrupt within the walls of a Parlament as well as of a citie; whereof in matters of neerest concernment all men will be judges; nor easily permitt, that the odds of voices in thir greatest councel, shall more endanger them by corrupt or credulous votes, then the odds of enemies by open assaults; judging that most voices ought not alwaies to prevail where main matters are in question. [CM, VI:114–15]

Here is the beginning of the wayfaring, coordinate or trailing style. Clause is piled upon clause, as though one can't quite portray this situation as fully governed by the Law of Nature, can't quite fashion and absorb it into patterned syntax and the rational order it reflects. Disaster was averted at this point, however, so Milton contemplates from a slight distance the headlong situation which would have resulted had Parliament agreed to the Treaty of Newport:

> And the dangers on either side they seriously thus waighd: from the treatie, short fruits of long labours and seaven years warr; securitie for twenty years, if we can hold it; reformation in the

church for three years: then put to shift again with our vanquishd
maister . . . bishops not totally remov'd, . . . thir lands alreadie
sold, not to be alienated, but rented, . . . delinquents few of many
brought to condigne punishment; accessories punishd. [CM, VI:
115]

In imagining what didn't happen then but almost certainly will now,
Milton employs an extremely loosened version of the coordinate style,
simply listing the provisions of the treaty. Signing it, that is, would
have meant the abject surrender of reasoned principle to irrational
sentiment, custom, and tradition.

This historical summary then concludes with a sketch of the Crom-
wellian period of heroic virtue and right reason:

Nor were thir actions less both at home and abroad then might
become the hopes of a glorious rising Commonwealth: nor were
the expressions both of armie and people, whether in thir pub-
lickdeclarations or several writings other then such as testifi'd
a spirit in this nation no less noble and well fitted to the liberty
of a Commonwealth then in the ancient Greeks or Romans. [CM,
VI:116][16]

This is balanced, shapely, high classic panegyric, far removed from
the dense thicket of menacing circumstances evoked only a few para-
graphs earlier. I would argue, therefore, that Milton subjects his
ready and easy rational plan to the pressures of political reality even
before he explicitly presents it. In keeping with the realistic and
pessimistic import of the tract's structure, its persona tends to make
inflated and exaggerated claims for the cause he espouses, the history in which he has participated, and the alternative future he is
proposing. Since he has just made the reader experience the dangers
and frustrations of actual political life as almost overwhelming, he
can lead him adequately to envision a nobler political order only by
ignoring such pressures and thereby acknowledging them.

The transition from historical survey to what is to be done in the
present situation is handled in a way that sharply juxtaposes the two
political alternatives, the two styles, and the overriding sense of futility that have already begun to emerge:

If by our ingratefull backsliding we make these [signal assistances
from heaven] fruitless; flying now to regal concessions from his
divine condescensions . . . making vain and viler then dirt the
blood of so many thousand faithfull and valiant English men, who
left us in this libertie, bought with thir lives; losing by a strange
aftergame of folly, all the battels we have wonn . . . treading back
again with lost labour all our happie steps in the progress of ref-

> ormation; and most pittifully depriving our selves the instant
> fruition of that free government which we have so dearly pur-
> chasd, a free Commonwealth, not only held by wisest men in all
> ages the noblest, the manliest, the equallest, the justest govern-
> ment, the most agreeable to all due libertie and proportiond
> equalitie, both human, civil, and Christian, most cherishing to
> vertue and true religion, but also . . . planely commended, or
> rather enioined by our Saviour himself. [CM, VI:118–19]

The first half of this quotation is another description and denunciation of the moral and practical consequences of restoring monarchical government, and once again momentum is transmitted from
participial to participial, consequence to consequence, until the
reader begins to experience the destruction of all principled human
aspiration and social organization. The passage then turns on the
clause, "and most pittifully depriving our selves the instant fruition
of that free government we have so dearly purchasd." The ensuing
apposition, "a free Commonwealth," brings the passage to a stand-
still, or at least it attempts to. The effect is that the speaker tries
to erect a dike to hold back the flood, but as he goes on to pile
superlative upon superlative, all framed by a "not only . . . but also"
construction, his voice acquires the now-familiar rhythm of uncon-
trolled momentum. Seeking to buttress the republican defenses
against catastrophe, he again acknowledges the near-omnipotence of
the forces responsible for the impending catastrophe.

The remainder of the pamphlet continues this movement back and
forth between these two apparent alternatives: the nation's surrender
to the logic of political reality or its ready and easy escape into a
condition of republican pure reason. The next two sections are the
ones analyzed in detail above, the long condemnation of monarchy
and popular slavishness, followed by the lucid outline of the free
commonwealth government. The latter introduces a defense of the
principle of a permanently enduring senate (CM, VI:126 ff.). Here
Milton is debating with the Harringtonians, who favor rotating the
members of the legislative body.[17] Since they are one of the few
rational groups left in England, this section is characterized by calm
argument and examination of the historical evidence. However, the
appeal to Harrington and his disciples is before long carried on in
the coordinate tones and rhythms of the polemical and pessimistic
sections of the tract:

> I see not therefor, how we can be advantag'd by successive and
> transitorie Parlaments; but that they are much likelier contin-
> ually to unsettle rather then to settle a free government; to
> breed commotions, changes, novelties and uncertainties; to

bring neglect upon present affairs and opportunities, while all
mindes are suspense with expectation of a new assemblie, and the
assemblie for a good space taken up with the new setling of it
self. [CM, VI:127]

However trenchant we may find this as an analysis of the vagaries of
elections and of periodically elected legislatures, it clearly derives
from an awareness of recent political history and contemporary political loyalties: the people cannot be relied upon to elect genuine republicans. This actual circumstance is the reason that imagined
circumstances are strung together in the quoted passage in a manner
that recalls all the speaker's direct responses to the current situation. As we have seen and will continue to see, royalist reality in-
vades the world of republican social reason even, and perhaps most
tellingly, when the republican persona works most determinedly to
shut it out.

The same rhetorical effect emerges from the description of the
electoral procedures Milton's plan might reluctantly tolerate. Elections would be designed gradually to exclude irrational elements of
society from the active body politic, and the speaker continues on to
suppose that a truly reformed citizenry would thereby be nurtured:

To make the people fittest to chuse, and the chosen fittest to
govern, will be to mend our corrupt and faulty education, to
teach the people faith not without vertue, temperance, modestie,
sobrietie, parsimonie, justice; not to admire wealth or honour;
to hate turbulence and ambition; to place every one his privat
welfare and happiness in the public peace, libertie and safetie.
[CM, VI:131—32]

Here again the speaker makes highly inflated claims for his plan,
listing the noble qualities that would be instilled in the populace, or-
ganizing the passage with a cadenced network of parallel infinitives,
rounding the discussion off quite elegantly. And here again the reader is given to understand that this ready and easy balance and harmony amounts to an admission of futility, a concentrated effort
temporarily to forget the obvious facts.[18]

Milton summarizes the ostensible impact of this section by claiming that "the way propounded is plane, easie and open before us; . . .
I say again, this way lies free and smooth before us" (CM, VI:133).
That these statements mean that the way is ready and easy only in an
imaginary world of pure reason is again emphasized in the next section (CM, VI:134ff.), in which a relatively calm analysis of monarchy
is soon interrupted by urgent and exasperated rhetorical questions:
"Can the folly be paralleld, . . . Shall we never grow old anough . . .

Is it such an unspeakable joy to serve, such felicitie to wear a yoke?"
(CM, VI:136). Finally Milton predicts in detail the kind of society his
plan would help to create, a society of religious liberty and opportunities for social advancement made possible by representative local
governments and courts and a vastly improved school system. This
fuller program is set forth in a style of careful and formal reasoning.
It begins with an assured definition of first principles: "The whole
freedom of man consists either in spiritual or civil libertie" (CM, VI:
141). After adapting to his present purposes the arguments on "spiritual libertie" he had published the year before, Milton presents his
ideas on local government and education:

> The other part of our freedom consists in the civil rights and
> advancements of every person according to his merit: the enjoy-
> ment of these never more certain, and the access to these never
> more open, then in a free Commonwealth. Both which in my
> opinion may be best and soonest obtaind, if every countie in the
> land were made a kinde of subordinate Commonaltie or Common-
> wealth . . . where the nobilitie and chief gentry . . . may build,
> houses or palaces, befitting thir qualitie, may bear part in the
> government, make thir own judicial laws, or use these that are,
> and execute them by thir own elected judicatures and judges
> without appeal, in all things of civil government between man
> and man. . . .
> They should have heer also schools and academies at thir
> own choice, wherin thir children may be bred up in thir own
> sight to all learning and noble education not in grammar only,
> but in all liberal arts and exercises. This would soon spread
> much more knowledge and civilitie, yea religion through all
> parts of the land, by communicating the natural heat of govern-
> ment and culture more distributively to all extreme parts,
> which now lie numm and neglected, would soon make the whole
> nation more industrious, more ingenuous at home, more potent,
> more honorable abroad. [CM, VI:143–44, 145]

Milton proposes no less than to transform the entire landscape of
England into an embodiment of pure reason. Despite the superbly
cool and collected tone, however, the syntax of these passages is
closer to the extended coordination of the polemical sections of the
tract than to the intricate and ample hybrids of looseness and suspension which K. G. Hamilton calls typically Miltonic. Here as
elsewhere in the tract the speaker makes no attempt to convey the
impression that his position successfully overrides that of his
opponents. The ready and easy amplitude of these sentences suggests instead that a rational republic would beget miniature repro-

ductions of itself as readily and easily as a monarchy generates triviality and degradation. The only difference is that monarchical potency functions in the real England of 1660; republicanism operates in an imaginary realm where all social forces would work for its success. Also it must be once more emphasized that the cool and collected rational tone moves toward sentimentality, particularly in the latter portion of the passage on a reformed school system. The parallel subjunctives and the rounded conclusion formed by the series of comparatives build into the passage an intimation that though the speaker may think he is proposing a practicable solution, he is in fact consoling himself with a private dream of social reason, one which might become a public reality, but not in this place at this time.[19]

It is clear that Milton's understanding of the political situation in which he is writing would not lead him to think that his plan might be accepted and implemented. He exploits the considerable resources of his prose rhetoric to convey just the opposite reading of current affairs. Directly in the polemical sections, indirectly in the proposing ones, he speaks "the last words of our expiring libertie" (CM, VI:148). This is most sharply and powerfully true of the concluding section, which begins ironically enough with a false statement: "I have no more to say at present" (CM, VI:147). About half of this concluding section is a suspended and massive sentence, too long to quote here, which duplicates the form of one discussed earlier (pp. 101-02): "But if the people be so affected . . . whatever new conceit now possesses us" (CM, VI:147-48). The analysis made of that previous sentence applies equally well to this one. The speaker makes a final heroic effort to contain the multitude of unreformed social conditions within a grand pattern of reason and principle, but as earlier, he finds it impossible to stop declaiming after the climactic predication, "our condition is not sound but rotten, both in religion and all civil prudence." He instead goes on to repeat his condemnations and dark predictions in summary form: "And will bring us soon, the way we are marching, to those calamities which attend alwaies and unavoidably on luxurie, all national judgments under forein or domestic slaverie: so far we shall be from mending our condition by monarchizing our government, whatever new conceit now possesses us." Such loose ends dangling from this recollection of Milton's warfaring prose style indicate that for now, at least, circumstance shall not be overcome. It would be dishonest, therefore, to end the tract on a positive note.

These then are the words with which Milton takes his leave of liberty:

But I trust I shall have spoken perswasion to abundance of sensible and ingenuous men: to som perhaps whom God may raise of these stones to become children of reviving libertie; and may reclaim, though they seem now chusing them a captain back for Egypt, to bethink themselves a little and consider whether they are rushing; to exhort this torrent also of the people, not to be so impetuos, but to keep thir due channell; and at length recovering and uniting thir better resolutions, now that they see alreadie how open and unbounded the insolence and rage is of our common enemies, to stay these ruinous proceedings; justly and timely fearing to what a precipice of destruction the deluge of this epidemic madness would hurrie us through the general defection of a misguided and abus'd multitude. [CM, VI:148–49]

This sentence embodies the organization of the entire pamphlet in intensified form. The primary syntax is simple, straightforward, and full of rational hope: "But I trust I shall have spoken perswasion to abundance of sensible and ingenuous men." But the virtually certain defeat of these hopes grows more and more evident in the long chain of dependent clauses added in the second edition, first in a parenthetical qualification, "though they seem now chusing them a captain back for Egypt," surrounded by the primary hopeful phrases, which themselves end with the dangerous participial, "rushing." The threatening implications of "rushing" are taken up by "this torrent also of the people, not to be so impetuos," but are restrained by "but to keep thir due channell." The participial clauses begin positively ("recovering and uniting . . ."), are interrupted by a longer, more threatening aside, "now that they see alreadie how open and unbounded the insolence and rage is of our common enemies," and can only partially recover with a phrase that ends with the words "ruinous proceedings." The final clause begins with brave adverbs, "justly and timely," but their impact is weakened by the governing participial they modify, "fearing," and is overwhelmed by a "deluge" of decisively bleak prepositional phrases: "to what a precipice of destruction the deluge of this epidemic madness would hurrie us through the general defection of a misguided and abus'd multitude."[20]

The struggle enacted in this final sentence, with the voice of reason slowly but surely turning into a voice bravely and honestly recognizing the true balance of political power, is the struggle enacted in the tract at large. My argument should not, however, be taken to mean that The Readie and Easie Way tells the story of a developing quietism or political cynicism in its author. Rather, what is most impressive within the stylistic and structural patterns I have outlined is the endurance of the speaker's commitment to a rational and free commonwealth. Despite his or Milton's forcefully communicated understanding of the immediate futility of republican ideas, he continues to the bitter end to challenge his audience: "But I trust I shall have spoken perswasion to abundance of sensible and ingenuous men." Only covertly through syntactic and structural ironies, after all, does Milton say republican politics have become impossible. Set against these ironies, his surface argument comes to mean that he retains some hope for the ultimate social realization of freedom and truth. Although Milton concludes his twenty years of political activism by arriving reluctantly at the political position announced in Paradise Lost, that "Tyranny must be" because "inordinate desires/And upstart Passions" will always "catch the Government from Reason," (XII, 85–96), he also brings these twenty years to an appropriate climax. What had always been the political weakness of Milton's prose, its inability to resolve the tension between regenerate principle and fallen circumstance, is turned into high political drama in the style and structure of The Readie and Easie Way.

CONCLUSION

In the course of the <u>Second Defence</u>, Milton interpreted his political and rhetorical career in his own inimitable and characteristic fashion:

> Since, then, I observed that there are, in all, three varieties of liberty without which civilized life is scarcely possible, namely ecclesiastical liberty, domestic or personal liberty, and civil liberty, and since I had already written about the first, while I saw that the magistrates were vigorously attending to the third, I took as my province the remaining one, the second or domestic kind. . . .
> Civil liberty, which was the last variety, I had not touched upon, for I saw that it was being adequately dealt with by the magistrates, nor did I write anything about the right of kings, until the king, having been declared an enemy by Parliament and vanquished in the field, was pleading his cause as a prisoner before the judges and was condemned to death. [IV:624, 626]

Speaking to a learned European audience, Milton imagines that since 1641 England has embarked not "in a troubl'd sea of noises and hoars disputes," but on a social adventure which is succeeding in realizing Christian liberty in all areas of social life. Each of his own works has been a judicious response to the configuration of social forces at that particular time. At the appropriate moments, he has participated in the successful agitations for ecclesiastical and civil liberty and initiated the struggle for domestic liberty. As Milton had always sought to do with the issues he wrote about, this highly patterned autobiography dignifies and uplifts his pamphleteering itself into a constellation of ideals.

Though I have argued that Milton's idealizing impulses constitute his political limitations, I have not intended to suggest that Milton should have compromised his views or made them less radical. Nor do I believe that by writing more in the manner of Lilburne and Walwyn, he would have guaranteed the reforms he sought in the divorce laws, or insured that most Englishmen would become republicans after 1649. What I do claim is that Milton did not translate his ideals into political terms. If his tracts were the only surviving documents of the English Revolution, we would know little about it as a major political event. Except for <u>Eikonoklastes</u>, and then through no fault of Milton's, these writings convey at best only a fragmentary sense of a political context. The reader must infer the answers to a series of

112

questions: What are the concrete issues? Which groups are con-
tending with which other groups? For whom is Milton speaking besides himself? The correct answer to this last question if of course
that Milton speaks not for other men but for truth, but this is a
politically dangerous distinction. We need only compare any of Milton's pamphlets with Swift's Drapier's Letters. The Drapier speaks
for the clear and present demands of Irishmen. If he advocates an
ideal of justice, he does so in the only way in which ideals make
sense in political discourse, as they emerge from concrete social
conditions and human needs. Milton is so imbued with principle and
so committed to it that, in his political prose, concepts and visions
do not emerge from a human context. They substitute for it. The
sense of political reality is most continuously and pervasively obscured in Milton's prose by his syntax. Sometimes open, sometimes
with difficulty closed, the form of Milton's sentences calls attention
to itself on page after page as an image of political engagement and
political dignity. Form embodies abstract ideal to the detriment of
concrete political meaning.[1]

It is often stated or implied that Milton's years of political activism were a regrettable digression from his true vocation as a poet.
A sophisticated form of this attitude is found in the contention that
"the ruin of Milton's political hopes precipitated him into his great-
est poetic achievements. Not the least of our debts to General Monck
and Charles II is that they were unwitting sponsors of Paradise Lost,
Paradise Regained, and Samson Agonistes. Milton learned from ad-
versity what prosperity could never have taught him."[2] It is unnecessary to base a reply to this argument on the fact that Milton almost
certainly began Paradise Lost before the Restoration.[3] Northrop
Frye's account of the relationship between the prose and Paradise
Lost is broadly acceptable:

> The Protestant in Milton fought for the restoration of the primi-
> tive church of the gospels, against the usurpation of tradition, or
> custom and error. The humanist in him fought for the ancient
> liberty of the Greek and Roman republics against the usurpation
> of kings and priests. The Parliamentarian in him fought for the
> liberties of the lords and commons against the usurpations of
> Star Chamber and royal prerogative. All these are causes
> rooted in history, models of the past to be recreated in the fu-
> ture. There is no evidence that Milton ceased to believe in any
> of these causes, but he was driven by a deeper logic than that of
> disillusionment to study the primal pattern, the ultimate myth of
> the gate of origin, the definitive insight into how things came to
> be, which Raphael gives Adam as the essence of his message and
> which Satan cuts off from himself. Milton's source told him that

        although heaven is a city and a society, the pattern established
        for man on earth by God was not social but individual, and not a
        city but a garden.[4]

Although Frye says that the creation of Paradise Lost was the result
of "a deeper logic than that of disillusionment," his discussion supports the view that Milton envisioned in his epic the pattern which
the Revolution failed to institute as an enduring historical reality.
He turned from politics back to poetry, but to epic poetry, a form
which allowed him to utilize more fruitfully the amplifying and uni-
versalizing tendencies he had nurtured through twenty years of pamphleteering. He now took not just divorce or censorship or political
dignity, but all reality as his province and transposed it into spacious
and principled vision.

    It will be observed that I am actually in agreement with the claim
that the Restoration not only released but inspired Milton to a truer
realization of his temperament and genius than he could achieve in
expository political discourse. But in my opinion, Milton's greatness
as a poet is inseparable from certain flaws in his political style; his
poetry relates to the prose not as alternative to alternative, but as
the logical outcome of the apolitical or antipolitical dimension of
Milton's revolutionary activism. The final sentence of the quotation
from Frye refers to the denouement of Paradise Lost, the "paradise
within thee, happier far," (XII, 587) which is the only and sufficient
defense against the historical realities so grimly adumbrated in
Books XI and XII.[5] And this returns us to what we have seen repeatedly in the course of the present study, the defiant individualism
of Milton's opinions and the spiritual or ideal character of his style
and argumentation. As much or more than he worked for social
change, Milton spent twenty years imagining his paradise within
while the social and political realm came increasingly—so it seemed
to him—to resemble the canvas painted in the final two books of his
epic. It is not surprising that a man of such a political temper would
become the propagandist of governments such as those of the Commonwealth and Protectorate. These were willed into existence by
one man, and "having destroyed the king's Englishmen and invented
God's Englishmen," they had to justify their actions and policies by
an ultimate, providential idealism.[6] Cromwell's regime implemented
ideas, as Milton's prose advocated them, in ways which severely re-
stricted the scope and depth of their relationships with the social order.

    Allen Grossman has summarized the points I am making here:

        Freedom depends on the moral autonomy of the reasoning indi-

vidual, but reason in Milton is bound up in the intensely personal
gesture of the gigantic rhetorician who, by mingling his will with
his discourse, summons a meaningful state of affairs rather than
defines its conditions. Milton's prose functions as a preemption
of reality rather than a description of it, and in this reflects the
limits also of the kind of poetry which he practices. His thematic
gigantism in poetry and hypotactic comprehensiveness in prose
suggest that for Milton psychic totalism is manipulated as an
argument against cosmic nihilism. . . . The limits of his poetic
style which Eliot saw very clearly and the limits of his rational
apologetic are seen in the effort, which Marvell intuited in him,
to exchange mind (as language) for world, rather than submit to
the evidences of final complexity in historical experience.[7]

To say that Milton, "by mingling his will with his discourse, summons
a meaningful state of affairs rather than defines its conditions" is to
say that the style of Milton's prose works relates to their content (or
rather, to the issues under consideration) in an authoritarian manner.
It is through his style, more particularly his "hypotactic comprehensiveness," that Milton imposes his will on the themes of his dis-
courses and, by extension, on the entire social and political context
in which he writes. Essentially, then, the politics of Milton's prose
style is the opposite of democratic. In the Leveller prose analyzed
in my first chapter, the relations between style and world are not
hierarchical and authoritarian. Style does not dominate world as it
does in Milton's prose. Rather, such relations are dialectical, mutual, equal. What has been said of George Orwell's writing can well
be applied to that of the Levellers, that it is "exemplary of a correct
way in which the moral sensibility, distrusting higher ambitions,
exercises its right to judge an imperfect world, never exempting itself from that world."[8] The politics of Leveller prose style is pre-
eminently democratic.

Every piece of discourse implies social relationships: between a
speaker and his audience, between an author and his material. The
style of every piece of discourse has therefore a politics. I propose
the following hypothesis as one of the laws in any systematic theory
of the politics of prose style: a style like Milton's which continuously
struggles to impose a literary pattern upon its materials is either
conservative in its political implications or, if the content of the
writing is reformist or progressive, it is unrealistic; a conversa-
tional and free-flowing style like that of the Levellers is the only
style truly suited to the advocacy of basic social change. The plausi-
bility of this hypothesis is indicated by the fact that the contrast between Milton and the Levellers can be observed in periods other than

the seventeenth century and in literary modes other than expository political prose.

For other historical periods, I choose to examine figures from the mid-nineteenth and mid-twentieth centuries. These periods were, like the mid-seventeenth century, times of political crisis and social turmoil. Thomas Carlyle, for example, is similar to Milton; he revered Oliver Cromwell as a "Hero" and wholeheartedly endorsed the Puritan Revolution. During the crisis of early industrialism in the 1840s, Carlyle in Past and Present denounced the cash nexus and proposed an authoritarian alternative to it in a tone and syntax raging as intensely for order as Milton's had. During the same decade, those who wrote on behalf of the Chartist movement advocated the Leveller program in the plain, familiar Leveller style. In the twentieth century the figure one might compare to Milton is Norman Mailer, who has prided himself on his individualism and independence of all left-wing groups, describing his own politics as a unique combination of Marx and Burke;[9] who hoped for a relationship between himself and John F. Kennedy similar to the one often imagined to have existed between Milton and Cromwell; and whose fictional works betray his ambition to write the definitive epic of the soul of America. The prose style of Mailer's books on the political happenings of the 1960s is marked by a convoluted and "hypotactic comprehensiveness" which has the same effect as in Milton: it diverts the reader's attention from the "final complexity in historical experience" to the dynamic personality and fertile mind of the author. The twentieth-century writer with the closest affinities to the Levellers and Chartists is Orwell. In his best work, such as Homage to Catalonia, Orwell regards his own character, opinions, and ideals as simply one important grouping of facts among many others comprising the totality of his discourse, all of which are to be fully sensed, intuited, and examined before judgments are to be passed and recommendations made.[10] In the nineteenth and twentieth centuries as in the seventeenth, in short, the high, intricate style of the literary intellectual fails where the low, straightforward style of the working-class leader[11] succeeds, at identifying problems and imagining solutions from a perspective which respects the contingencies of actual social and political experience.

The more involved and elaborate the prose style, the more conservative the social meaning, and vice versa: I find that this is also true in the area of nineteenth-century prose fiction. The later novels of Henry James constitute perhaps the most extreme example. To this reader at least, the extreme complication of James's prose syntax helps to effect a drastic narrowing of the social range of his fiction. His wealthy, leisured, and exquisitely discriminating protagonists are an elite, of sorts, who seem to have found their proper home in the well-wrought elaboration and sophistication of Jamesian prose. If we recall the close association between traditional social hierarchies, and traditional hierarchies of literary style, we can construct the following description of the relationship between James's novels and traditional hierarchical literature: Just as James's prose style is less robust and vigorous, and even more elaborate, than the traditional high style of tragedy and epic, so do James's protagonists exist divorced from the leadership functions and responsibilities in the social hierarchy which their ruling class ancestors executed with such strenuous and heroic grandeur. Sharply contrasting fictional procedures are to be found in nineteenth-century realism. The novels in this tradition are written in a manner which subordinates words to things and, at its best, thereby creates in the reader "the flush of enchantment with the host of real events which form our lives."[12] Although I know his works only in translation, the novelist who comes most forcefully and vividly to mind in this regard is Tolstoy. Here again it seems that a relatively simple and direct mode of utterance facilitates serious encounters with social situations, social questions, and broad movements of social forces. Georg Lukács's thesis in Studies in European Realism that, socially and politically speaking, the great realistic novels are all inherently progressive—whatever the avowed politics of their authors—parallels my argument for the egalitarian implications of plainspoken expository political prose.[13]

The most interesting of all these contrasts to consider in relation to the hypothesis I am advancing is one that is fundamental to Erich Auerbach's vast study of Mimesis, the one Auerbach draws between the stylistic and social hierarchies of pagan antiquity and the plain, potentially revolutionary seriousness of New Testament writing. As implied above in my remarks on James, the high style of tragedy and epic derives from the classical theory of separation of styles, and this means that it derives from and serves as ideological justification for a static, hierarchical society:

> Everything commonly realistic, everything pertaining to everyday life, must not be treated on any level except the comic, which admits no problematic probing. As a result the boundaries of realism are narrow. And if we take the word realism a little more strictly, we are forced to conclude that there could be no serious literary treatment of everyday occupations and social classes—merchants, artisans, peasants, slaves—of everyday scenes and places—home, shop, field, store—of everyday customs and institutions—marriage, children, work, earning a living —in short, of the people and its life.[14]

In other words, the high style was inseparable from a condescending attitude toward "the people and its life." If one can identify the prose styles of Milton, Carlyle, and Mailer as the expository descendants of the classical high style, then one can find the conservative political implications of these styles confirmed by their conservative social origins.

As Auerbach points out, the low style for which this doctrine provides is not common or plain speech but is instead another means by which the aristocracy condescends to the populace. But there is another kind of low style which Auerbach is at pains to describe and define throughout his book, a style which can bestow serious literary treatment upon common life and which is therefore deeply subversive of the doctrine of separation of styles and the social hierarchy from which this doctrine derives. In the course of an argument that this potentially radical style originated in the Judaeo-Christian tradition, Auerbach interprets as follows the version of Peter's denial of Christ given in the Gospel according to Saint Mark:

> The visual and sensory as it appears here is no conscious imitation and hence it is rarely completely realized. It appears because it is attached to the events which are to be related, because it is revealed in the demeanor and speech of profoundly stirred individuals and no effort need be devoted to the task of elaborating it. . . . The author of the Gospel according to St. Mark has no viewpoint which would permit him to present a factual, objective portrait of, let us say, the character of Peter. He is at the core of what goes on; he observes and relates only what matters in relation to Christ's presence and mission; and in the present case it does not even occur to him to tell us how the incident ended, that is, how Peter got away. . . . Without any effort on his part, as it were, and purely through the inner movement of what he relates, the story becomes visually concrete. and the story speaks to everybody; everybody is urged and indeed required to take sides for or against it. [15]

I submit that the plain and serious voice of the Gospels, bespeaking solidarity with common life, corresponds in its discursive characteristics and in its egalitarian social bearings to the political voices of the Levellers, the Chartists, and George Orwell.

Those whose primary and ongoing experiences occur among the books and traditions of Western culture, those who are intellectually sophisticated and aesthetically ambitious are perhaps also those who are most often given to writing in the elaborate, high style which I am arguing is inherently authoritarian and conservative. Yet we also know from Raymond Williams and others that literary intellectuals of this sort have in the modern era repeatedly and urgently demanded social change.[16] Since the medium of these demands, the high style, has frequently contradicted the demands themselves, relationships between literary intellectuals and the larger movements for social change have usually been at best ambivalent, at worst mutually frustrating. Milton remains interesting to us as an intellectual and artist in politics because his political life is the first major example of this disquieting phenomenon. The English Revolution, which generated to one degree or another the entire spectrum of later political parties, can be seen as the beginning of modern politics. The more secular and radical participants in the Revolution helped create modern English prose. It is at least possible to contend that the programs and styles of Lilburne, Walwyn, and Winstanley offered a means of realizing the open-ended progress Milton so magnificently foresaw in Areopagitica. That Milton found it necessary to disavow this city and society and commit himself instead to a suprapolitical garden is to my way of thinking no cause for satisfaction. But we can at least be grateful that in his recoil from political disappointment Milton's idealism remained substantial enough for him to take us back to that garden and give us the choice of building our collective life there.

NOTES

Introduction

1 The present volume was substantially completed before I had the opportunity to read Achievements of the Left Hand: Essays on the Prose of John Milton, ed. Michael Lieb and John T. Shawcross (Amherst: University of Massachusetts Press, 1974). The essays in that collection most pertinent to the questions I will be pursuing here are the following: Joseph Anthony Wittreich, Jr., "'The Crown of Eloquence': The Figure of the Orator in Milton's Prose Works," pp. 3–54; Michael Lieb, "Milton's Of Reformation and the Dynamics of Controversy," pp. 55–82; and Harry Smallenburg, "Government of the Spirit: Style, Structure, and Theme in Treatise of Civil Power," pp. 219–38. See also by Smallenburg, "Milton's Cosmic Sentences," Language and Style 5 (1971–72): 108–14.

2 Northrop Frye, The Return of Eden (Toronto: University of Toronto Press, 1965), p. 115.

3 This pattern of motivation has been explored at length in William Haller, The Rise of Puritanism (New York: Columbia University Press, 1938), pp. 305–23; Arthur E. Barker, Milton and the Puritan Dilemma, 1641–1660 (Toronto: University of Toronto Press, 1941), pp. 3–18; and Joan Webber, The Eloquent "I": Style and Self in Seventeenth-Century Prose (Madison: University of Wisconsin Press, 1968), pp. 199 ff.

4 John Holloway, The Victorian Sage (London: Macmillan & Co., 1953).

5 A Collection of Essays by George Orwell (New York: Anchor Books, 1954), p. 163.

6 These terms are used extensively in Frank Brady, "Prose Style and the 'Whig' Tradition," Bulletin of the New York Public Library 66 (1962): 455–63.

Chapter 1

1 For Croll, see the collection by J. Max Patrick et al., Style, Rhetoric, and Rhythm: Essays by Morris W. Croll (Princeton: Princeton University Press, 1966). Most of the subsequent studies have been concerned with conscious literary movements in which Milton did not participate. See among others those of R. F. Jones et al., The Seventeenth Century: Studies in the History of English Thought and Literature from Bacon to Pope (Palo Alto: Stanford University Press, 1951); Robert Adolph, The Rise of Modern Prose Style (Cambridge, Mass.: M.I.T. Press, 1968); and Earl Miner, "Patterns of Stoicism in Thought and Prose Styles, 1530–1700," PMLA 85 (1970): 1023–34. The present study relies throughout upon Croll's discussion of the loose style, in "The Baroque Style in Prose," Style, Rhetoric, and Rhythm, pp. 207–33.

Although the evidence Miner has collected seriously questions some aspects of Croll's general view of seventeenth-century literary history, I do not think his article warrants "laying aside" (Miner, p. 1033) Croll's highly imaginative analyses of prose syntax.

2 It seems likely that in the first passage quoted here, Milton was thinking not only of the Fathers, but also of a variety of excesses in Elizabethan and seventeenth-century prose, including "the intricat, and involv'd sentences" often characteristic of the loose style.

3 George Williamson, The Senecan Amble: A Study in Prose Form from Bacon to Collier (Chicago: University of Chicago Press, 1951), p. 213 and n. 3.

4 K. G. Hamilton, "The Structure of Milton's Prose," in Language and Style in Milton: A Symposium in Honor of the Tercentenary of "Paradise Lost," ed. Ronald D. Emma and John T. Shawcross (New York: Frederick Ungar, 1967), p. 313. Richard Weaver, however, agrees with C. E. Vaughan's emphasis on the linear form of Milton's sentences. They are "shaped as the driving force of the thought requires," The Ethics of Rhetoric (Chicago: Henry Regnery Co., 1953), p. 144.

5 L. C. Martin, ed., Sir Thomas Browne: Religio Medici and Other Works (Oxford: Oxford University Press, 1964), p. 3.

6 This passage is used for different purposes in Leonard Nathanson, The Strategy of Truth: A Study of Sir Thomas Browne (Chicago: University of Chicago Press, 1967), pp. 82–86.

7 On both appositions and trailing clauses, see Croll, Style, Rhetoric, and Rhythm, p. 224.

8 Croll, Style, Rhetoric, and Rhythm, p. 208: "[The anti-Ciceronian movement] preferred the forms that express the energy and labor of minds seeking the truth, not without dust and heat, to the forms that express a contented sense of the enjoyment and possession of it."

9 Richard Hooker, Of the Laws of Ecclesiastical Polity, 2 vols. (New York: Everyman, 1965), I:190–91.

10 In "Notes on Hooker's Prose," RES 15 (1939): 195–96, D. C. Boughner comments on Hooker's sense of rhythm and his "careful use of connective tissue" (here the "unto whom . . . by them" construction).

11 Ibid., p. 195.

12 It should be noted in passing that Milton agrees with Hooker about human inequality but differs significantly from him in his estimate of the people's capacity freely to choose as their governors men of "wisdome and integritie." Within a year (see below, pp. 26 and 123, n. 23) Milton was to lose a political faith which may seem naive but which at least confronts a problem left nicely obscure in Hooker's discussion by his orchestration of lovely prose harmonies: If "them who are to be governed" are in "the opinion of very great and judicious men . . . of a servile disposition," how can they "assent" to be governed by "the noble, wise, and virtuous"? How indeed can they make choices at all?

13 See William Haller, ed., Tracts on Liberty in the Puritan Revolution, 3 vols. (New York: Columbia University Press, 1934), I:128–39; and

William R. Parker, Milton's Contemporary Reputation (Columbus: Ohio State University Press, 1940), pp. 12–44.

14 See Godfrey Davies and William Haller, eds., The Leveller Tracts: 1647–1653 (New York: Columbia University Press, 1944), pp. 8, 35–37, 40–41, 48–49.

15 Davies and Haller, Leveller Tracts, pp. 20, 27, report that Milton was ordered by the Council of State to reply to one of the Leveller manifestos, The Second Part of Englands New Chains Discovered, but that he never did. They also quote, p. 32, Lilburne's favorable reference to a passage in the First Defence in which Milton admonishes Cromwell to uphold liberty. See also Don M. Wolfe, "Lilburne's Note on Milton," MLN 56 (1941): 360–63.

16 Davies and Haller, Leveller Tracts, pp. 406–09.

17 Webber, Eloquent "I", p. 60.

18 See Webber, Eloquent "I", p. 61. The emergence of Lilburne's political principles from his concrete encounters with injustice is described in Don M. Wolfe, Milton in the Puritan Revolution (New York: Thomas Nelson and Sons, 1941), pp. 142–47.

19 Davies and Haller, Leveller Tracts, p. 140.

20 Christopher Hill, The Century of Revolution: 1603–1714 (New York: Norton, 1966), pp. 126–27. The remainder of the present chapter relies heavily on Hill's interpretation of the revolutionary decades, pp. 119–44.

21 A. S. P. Woodhouse, ed., Puritanism and Liberty, Being the Army Debates (Chicago: University of Chicago Press, 1951), pp. 53–54.

22 Christopher Hill, The World Turned Upside Down: Radical Ideas during the English Revolution (New York: Viking Press, 1972), p. 324. In the passage from which this description of Cromwell is extracted, Hill draws a parallel between Milton and Cromwell similar to the one I am developing: "Milton . . . combined radical intellectual convictions with patrician social prejudices, rather as Oliver Cromwell combined some genuinely radical religious beliefs with the normal social assumptions of a country gentleman."

23 Eikon Basilike was published sixty times in 1649, Eikonoklastes only twice. See Francis F. Madan, A New Bibliography of the "Eikon Basilike" of King Charles the First (London: Quaritch, 1950), pp. 2–4. Summarized in PW, III:150.

Chapter 2

1 Everett N. Emerson, in The Prose of John Milton, ed. J. Max Patrick (New York: Anchor Books, 1967), p. 38.

2 Barker, Puritan Dilemma, p. 22.

3 See ibid., p. 50.

4 See William Haller, "John Foxe and the Puritan Revolution," in Jones, The Seventeenth Century, pp. 222–23.

5 In Fred E. Ekfelt, "The Graphic Diction of Milton's English Prose,"

PQ 25 (1946): 66. See also Joshua H. Neumann, "Milton's Prose Vocabulary," PMLA 60 (1945): 102–12.

6 Hamilton, "Structure of Milton's Prose," p. 329.

7 See ibid., p. 308; and Weaver, Ethics of Rhetoric, p. 146, for additional comment on this introductory vision.

8 "The Typology of Paradise Regained," MP 53 (1956): 234; reprinted in Milton: Modern Essays in Criticism, ed. Arthur E. Barker (New York: Oxford University Press, 1965), p. 439; and in Frye, The Return of Eden, p. 133.

9 Webber, Eloquent "I", p. 194.

10 Employing an approach similar to the one developed in Surprised by Sin: The Reader in "Paradise Lost" (New York: St. Martin's Press, 1967), Stanley E. Fish has recently demonstrated that this tract is written in a way that exposes the inadequacy and deceitfulness of its own apparent rationality. Fish confines himself, however, to the tract's polemical dimension. See "Reasons that Imply Themselves: Image, Argument, and the Reader in Milton's Reason of Church Government," in Seventeenth-Century Imagery: Essays on Uses of Figurative Language from Donne to Farquhar, ed. Earl Miner (Berkeley: University of California Press, 1971), pp. 83–102. A revised version appears in Fish, Self-Consuming Artifacts: The Experience of Seventeenth-Century Literature (Berkeley: University of California Press, 1972), pp. 265–302.

11 See Webber, Eloquent "I", p. 202.

12 Ciceronian, at least according to Hamilton's definition: "The idea is introduced, then explained and qualified through a complex of closely integrated dependent clauses, before being completed or resolved only as the sentence comes to an end." "Structure," p. 308.

13 I find Fish's discussion of the antirational impact of Milton's preface the least convincing part of his essay. See "Reasons That Imply Themselves," pp. 89–91; Self-Consuming Artifacts, pp. 265–71.

14 C. S. Lewis finds in this passage the "central paradox" of Milton's general vision: "Discipline, while the world is yet unfallen, exists for the sake of what seems its very opposite—for freedom, almost for extravagance . . . The happy soul is, like a planet, a wandering star; yet in that very wandering (as astronomy teaches) invariable; she is eccentric beyond all predicting, yet equable in her eccentricity. The heavenly frolic arises from an orchestra which is in tune; the rules of courtesy make perfect ease and freedom possible between those who obey them. Without sin, the universe is a Solemn Game: and there is no good game without rules." A Preface to Paradise Lost (Oxford: Oxford University Press, 1942), p. 81.

15 PW, I:817, n. 115. The allusion is to Philippians 4:8.

16 Webber provides a discussion of the autobiographical aspects of the digression in Eloquent "I", pp. 193–99.

17 The assertion is made by Ralph A. Haug, PW, I:740.

18 William R. Parker, Milton: A Biography, 2 vols. (Oxford: Oxford
    University Press, 1968), I:223.
19 The third sentence also has a harmonious cadence: "A surer sign of
    his lost shame he could not have given, then seeking thus unseasonably
    to prepossesse men of his modesty."
20 This greater fluency qualifies Webber's idea that the eulogy's function
    is analogous to that of the personal digression in The Reason of Church
    Government. See Eloquent "I", p. 206.

Chapter 3

1 Helen Darbishire, ed., Early Lives of Milton (London: Constable,
   1932), life by Edward Phillips, p. 63. Quoted in Barker, Puritan Dilemma, pp. 63–64.
2 Barker, Puritan Dilemma, p. 63.
3 See Northrop Frye, The Well-Tempered Critic (Bloomington: Indiana
   University Press, 1963), pp. 41–42: "The ego has no interest in communication, but only in expression."
4 For a discussion of Milton's "idea of matrimony," and the ways in
   which it diverges from Puritan orthodoxy on the subject, see John
   Halkett, Milton and the Idea of Matrimony (New Haven: Yale University Press, 1970), pp. 1–97.
5 In "Hail Wedded Love," ELH 13 (1946): 80, 92–93. See also Frye,
   The Return of Eden, p. 115: "Domestic liberty, the goal of human
   development itself, takes us from dialectic to the emblematic vision
   or parable, and requires a poet."
6 Dr. Johnson, no friend of Milton's radical prose, was to take this low
   road: "In a man whose opinion of his own merit was like Milton's,
   less provocation might have raised violent resentment. Milton soon
   determined to repudiate Mary Powell for disobedience; and, being one
   of those who could easily find arguments to justify inclination, published (in 1644) The Doctrine and Discipline of Divorce; which was
   followed by The Judgement of Martin Bucer concerning Divorce; and
   the next year, his Tetrachordon, Expositions upon the Four Chief
   Places of Scripture which Treat of Marriage." The Works of Samuel
   Johnson, 12 vols. (London: J. Nichols & Son, 1810), IX:103.
7 This passage suggests some of the reasons Milton might hesitate to
   ally himself with the Levellers.
8 See PW, II:142; and Parker, Milton, I:263–64.
9 See Parker, Milton, I:264–66.
10 It is of course one of the decorums of the deliberative oration that the
   speaker present himself in a formal self-portrait. See PW, II:172;
   and Wilbur Gilman, Milton's Rhetoric: Studies in the Defense of Liberty (Columbia: University of Missouri Press, 1939), p. 17, for discussions of Milton's adherence to this convention in Areopagitica.
11 Hamilton, "Structure of Milton's Prose," p. 329.
12 For a catalogue of the major image patterns in the tract, see Alan F.

Price, "Incidental Imagery in Areopagitica," MP 49 (1952): 217–22. Obviously, I am arguing that the imagery is far from incidental. This argument is made in a somewhat different fashion in John X. Evans, "Imagery as Argument in Milton's Areopagitica," TSLL 8 (1966–67): 189–205.

13 I mean something rather different from the conventional pattern of the deliberative oration, to which Areopagitica rigorously adheres. On this structure, see PW, II:158–71; and Gilman, Milton's Rhetoric, pp. 9–44.

14 For an interpretation of Areopagitica which starts from the tract's relationships with Isocrates and Saint Paul, see Joseph Anthony Wittreich, Jr., "Milton's Areopagitica: Its Isocratic and Ironic Contexts," Milton Studies 4 (1972): 101–15. For an altogether contrasting treatment of the oration, see John Illo, "The Misreading of Milton," Columbia University Forum 8, no. 2 (Spring, 1965), 38–42; reprinted in Radical Perspectives in the Arts, ed. Lee Baxandall (Baltimore: Penguin Books, 1972), pp. 178–92. Illo stresses the denial of toleration to Roman Catholics and most Anglicans and overestimates, I believe, Milton's affinities with twentieth-century revolutionaries. A similarly misleading emphasis on the intolerant aspects of the oration is to be found in Willmoore Kendall, "How to Read Milton's Areopagitica," Journal of Politics 22 (1960): 439–73.

15 See Barker, Puritan Dilemma, pp. 78, 88. Sirluck analyzes in considerable detail Milton's attempts to influence these realities on a more immediate level. The arguments presented in Areopagitica were designed, Sirluck argues, to encourage Erastian sentiment in Parliament and thereby strengthen parliamentary opposition to the Westminster Assembly. See PW, II:173–78.

Chapter 4

1 David Masson, The Life of John Milton, 7 vols. (London: Macmillan & Co., 1859–94), IV:76. Quoted in PW, III:105.

2 See Parker, Milton, I:346.

3 These and other circumstances which prompted Cromwell to put the king on trial are analyzed in Wolfe, Puritan Revolution, pp. 189–93.

4 See PW, III:136.

5 See PW, III:107, 131–32.

6 P. A. Duhamel, "Milton's Alleged Ramism," PMLA 67 (1952): 1052. Quoted in PW, III:131.

7 Milton's interpretation of this evidence has been defended in Hughes, "Milton's Treatment of Reformation History in The Tenure of Kings and Magistrates," in Jones, The Seventeenth Century, pp. 247–63.

8 Barker, Puritan Dilemma, pp. 300, 137, 156, 196.

9 PW, III:139. See also Richard Weaver's statement, Ethics of Rhetoric, p. 161, that Milton was "consistently a writer of substance" who took a "magisterial" attitude toward language.

10 See Barker, Puritan Dilemma, p. 162.

11 This argument, the primary thesis of both antimonarchical tracts, was doubtless one of the sources of Milton's characterization of God and Satan in Paradise Lost. God is the only legitimate king, the constitutional monarch par excellence, obedient to the lawful parliament of his own Being. Satan, having rebelled against this divine constitution, installs himself as the absolute monarch of hell, surrounded by his Cavalier court. Without referring to the antimonarchical tracts, Frye takes a similar view of Satan in The Return of Eden, p. 106.

12 This allegory called down upon Milton's politics the wrath of S. B. Liljegren, who saw Milton in it "constituting himself one of the few righteous joined in hatred, contempt, and irresponsibility against the greater part of the English people at the Revolution." Studies in Milton (New York: Haskell House, 1967), p. 143. Liljegren was not entirely wrong.

13 Cf. S. R. Gardiner, History of the Commonwealth and Protectorate, 3 vols. (London: Longmans, Green & Co., 1897—1901), I:195—96: "In such a case mere negative criticism avails but little. What was needed was the development of a higher loyalty to the nation in the place of the lower loyalty to the King, and the quickening of a sense of the exuberant vitality of the collective life of the people in the place of devotion to the head of the national organization. Time had been when Milton had struck that key, and gazed on a vision of a 'noble and puissant nation rousing herself like a strong man after sleep and shaking her invincible locks.' He could not speak in that strain of a Commonwealth supporting itself on an armed force." Quoted in Wolfe, Puritan Revolution, p. 222.

14 See PW, III:344; and Zera S. Fink, "The Development of Milton's Political Thought," PMLA 57 (1942): 731.

15 See PW, III:581, 582 for other such tirades inserted into the second edition.

16 Ernest Sirluck, "Milton's Political Thought: The First Cycle," MP 61 (1964): 213.

Chapter 5

1 The evolution of Milton's attitude toward "the people" is outlined in Wolfe, Puritan Revolution, pp. 249—52, 256—58, and 261—66.

2 See Barker, Puritan Dilemma, pp. 156—214.

3 In The Restoration of Charles II, 1658—1660 (San Marino: The Huntington Library, 1955), Godfrey Davies provides a detailed account of the context of Milton's final political gestures.

4 Parker, Milton, I:519.

5 Patrick, ed., The Prose of John Milton, p. 443.

6 This view of the style of Paradise Regained, although not necessarily this view of its implications, is taken in Louis L. Martz, The Paradise Within: Studies in Vaughan, Traherne, and Milton (New Haven: Yale University Press, 1964), pp. 171—77.

7 For an extended discussion of these final weeks of the Revolution, see Davies, The Restoration, pp. 256–337.

8 See CM, VI:358–59, including the textual notes to p. 111 on p. 359.

9 In Be Merry and Wise, Or A Seasonable Word (London; 16 March 1660), p. 6, Roger L'Estrange was much amused at the way events were exposing Milton's predicament: "I could only wish his Excellency [Monck] had been a little civiller to Mr. Milton; for, just as he had finished his Model of a Commonwealth directing in these very terms, the Choyce MEN NOT ADDICTED TO A SINGLE PERSON, OR HOUSE OF LORDS, AND THE WORK IS DONE. In come the secluded Members, and spoyl his Project." Quoted in Wolfe, Puritan Revolution, p. 236.

10 Fink, "Development of Milton's Political Thought," pp. 708, 734, 736.

11 Barbara K. Lewalski, "Milton: Political Beliefs and Polemical Methods, 1659–60," PMLA 74 (1959): 191–202. See especially pp. 196–97.

12 For an analysis of the place of Milton's republicanism in the spectrum of antiroyalist positions current in the final months before the Restoration, see Barker, Puritan Dilemma, pp. 269–90. Barker finds that Milton's thought is closest to the theocratic views of the Fifth Monarchists, but that Milton remained distinct from this and other such groups by his continued insistence on a harmony between rational humanism and Christian regeneration in the republican and theocratic elite.

13 E. N. S. Thompson, "Milton's Prose Style," PQ 14 (1935): 5.

14 On warfaring and wayfaring, see PW, II:515 and n. 102.

15 These structural divisions are not as clear-cut as my discussion may suggest. Brief statements contrasting the republican plan with what is actually happening appear now and then in the polemical sections: "Wheras in a free Commonwealth, any governor or chief counselor offending, may be remov'd and punishd without the least commotion . . . The happiness of a nation must needs be firmest and certainest in a full and free Councel of thir own electing, where no single person, but reason only swaies." (CM, VI:121–22) The arrangement of key terms in these sentences suggests the rational stability of the proposed government. In the first sentence, "free Commonwealth" stands guard over the potentially tumultuous verbs, "offending . . . remov'd and punishd," until the danger of conflict is ruled out in the final phrase. The second sentence moves in an orderly manner from effect to efficient cause to final cause: "The happiness of a nation . . . a full and free Councel of thir own electing . . . where . . . reason only swaies."

16 True to himself to the end, Milton bestows all praise for the right reason upon his own Defences. This passage continues as follows: "Nor was the heroic cause unsuccessfully defended to all Christendom against the tongue of a famous and thought invincible adversarie; nor the constancie and fortitude that so nobly vindicated our liberty, our victory at once against two the most prevailing usurpers over mankinde, superstition and tyrannie unpraisd or uncelebrated in a written

monument, likely to outlive detraction, as it hath hitherto convinc'd or silenc'd not a few of our detractors, especially in parts abroad."

17 For detailed comparisons of the governments proposed by Milton and Harrington, see Wolfe, Puritan Revolution, pp. 304–10; and Barker, Puritan Dilemma, pp. 265–69.

18 Wolfe, Puritan Revolution, p. 239, summarizes as follows the judgment passed on The Readie and Easie Way in The Censure of the Rota (London, 26 March 1660): "In his governmental notions Milton never descends to particulars; his head is always in the clouds."

19 Granting the accuracy of Lewalski's analysis (see above, p. 99) I find it difficult to believe that Milton seriously expected or even hoped that the revisions he made for the second edition would help to fashion a republican coalition. The primary impact of these revisions is to clarify the alternating rhetorical rhythm I have outlined. The two editions may be compared by consulting the textual notes in CM, VI:359ff.

20 The phrase, "to som perhaps whom God may raise of these stones to become children of reviving libertie," is no doubt a reference to the words of John the Baptist at Matthew 3:7–9 and Luke 3:8: "I say unto you, that God is able of these stones to raise up children of Abraham." Louis L. Martz has pointed out to me that this phrase and the ensuing references to flood waters may also constitute an allusion to Metamorphoses, I, 381–415, in which Deucalion and Pyrrha repopulate the world after the Flood by casting stones behind them. Both references would suggest, in line with my argument, that Milton does not expect the English political situation to improve without miraculous divine intervention.

Conclusion

1 By careful inspection of the arguments used in Areopagitica, Sirluck has demonstrated that Milton was capable of interpreting a specific political situation with considerable shrewdness. See above, chap. 3, n. 15. That Milton retained this ability to the end of his life I have attempted to show in my preface and notes to Of True Religion, forthcoming in PW, VIII. Yet the point remains that this level of discourse is not self-evident; it must be painstakingly interpreted by the modern editor. The surface rhetoric of both these tracts is for the most part generalized and idealistic.

2 These comments were made by Professor George Lord in evaluating an earlier draft of this study. I am indebted to Mr. Lord for provoking the remainder of this conclusion. A brief analysis of Milton's political career written from a similar point of view has recently appeared: H. R. Trevor-Roper, "The Elitist Politics of Milton," TLS, no. 3717 (1 June, 1973): 601–03. Trevor-Roper makes in a tone of dismissal some of the same points I have been attempting to explore.

3 Parker, Milton, I:508–10, II:1064–65. Parker's contention (I:313–22,

II:903–17) that <u>Samson</u> was written in the 1640s has not gained general acceptance.

4 Frye, <u>The Return of Eden</u>, pp. 113–14.
5 On the exemplary individual voice of the narrator in the major poems, see Martz, <u>The Paradise Within</u>, pp. 103–201; Anne D. Ferry, <u>Milton's Epic Voice: The Narrator in "Paradise Lost"</u> (Cambridge, Mass.: Harvard University Press, 1963); and William G. Riggs, <u>The Christian Poet in "Paradise Lost"</u> (Berkeley: University of California Press, 1972).
6 See Allen Grossman, "Milton's Sonnet 'On the Late Massacre in Piemont': A Note on the Vulnerability of Persons in a Revolutionary Situation," in <u>Literature in Revolution</u>, ed. Charles Newman and George Abbot White, a special issue of <u>Triquarterly</u> 23–24 (1972): 296.
7 Grossman, "Milton's Sonnet," 294–95.
8 Stanley Cavell, <u>Must We Mean What We Say?</u> (New York: Scribner's, 1969), p. 303 n.
9 Mailer, <u>The Armies of the Night</u> (New York: New American Library, 1968), pp. 111–13, 204–13.
10 For these and for some of the preceding comments on Mailer, I am indebted to a seminar paper on Mailer, Orwell, and George Jackson by Diana M. Smith.
11 Orwell was of course not a working class leader, but books like <u>Down and Out in Paris and London</u> and <u>The Road to Wigan Pier</u> reveal that he went to considerable trouble to absorb as much as he could of working-class experience.
12 George Dennison, <u>The Lives of Children</u> (New York: Random House, 1969), p. 277.
13 On Tolstoy specifically, see Lukács, <u>Studies in European Realism</u> (New York: Grosset and Dunlap, 1964), pp. 126–205.
14 Erich Auerbach, <u>Mimesis: The Representation of Reality in Western Literature</u> (Princeton: Princeton University Press, 1953), p. 27.
15 Auerbach, <u>Mimesis</u>, pp. 41–42.
16 See Raymond Williams, <u>Culture and Society, 1780–1950</u> (New York: Columbia University Press, 1958), passim.

BIBLIOGRAPHY

Only works of particular significance in the immediate intellectual history of this book are listed here.

Primary Sources

Davies, Godfrey, and Haller, William, eds. The Leveller Tracts: 1647–1653. New York: Columbia University Press, 1944.

Haller, William, ed. Tracts on Liberty in the Puritan Revolution, 3 vols. New York: Columbia University Press, 1934.

Hooker, Richard. Of the Laws of Ecclesiastical Polity, 2 vols. New York: Everyman edition, 1965.

Martin, L. C., ed. Sir Thomas Browne: Religio Medici and Other Works. Oxford: Oxford University Press, 1964.

Patterson, Frank Allen et al. eds. The Works of John Milton, 18 vols. New York: Columbia University Press, 1931–38.

Wolfe, Don M. et al. eds. Complete Prose Works of John Milton, 8 vols. New Haven: Yale University Press, 1953–

Puritanism and the Puritan Revolution

Davies, Godfrey. The Restoration of Charles II, 1658–1660. San Marino: The Huntington Library, 1955.

Haller, William. Liberty and Reformation in the Puritan Revolution. New York: Columbia University Press, 1955.

———. The Rise of Puritanism. New York: Columbia University Press, 1938.

Hill, Christopher. The Century of Revolution, 1603–1714. New York: Thomas Nelson and Sons, 1961.

———. Intellectual Origins of the English Revolution. Oxford: Oxford University Press, 1965.

———. Puritanism and Revolution: Studies in Interpretation of the English Revolution of the 17th Century. London: Martin Secker & Warburg, 1958.

———. Society and Puritanism in Pre-Revolutionary England. Oxford: Oxford University Press, 1964.

Prose Style

Brady, Frank. "Prose Style and the 'Whig' Tradition." Bulletin of the New York Public Library 66 (1962): 455–63.

Croll, Morris W. Style, Rhetoric, and Rhythm: Essays by Morris W. Croll, ed. J. Max Patrick et al. Princeton: Princeton University Press, 1966.

Hamilton, K. G. The Two Harmonies: Poetry and Prose in the Seven-
teenth Century. Oxford: Oxford University Press, 1963.
Jones, R. F. et al. The Seventeenth Century: Studies in the History of
English Thought and Literature from Bacon to Pope. Palo Alto: Stan-
ford University Press, 1951.
Orwell, George. "Politics and the English Language." In A Collection of
Essays by George Orwell. New York: Anchor Books, 1954, pp. 162–77.
Webber, Joan. The Eloquent "I": Style and Self in Seventeenth-Century
Prose. Madison: University of Wisconsin Press, 1968.
Williamson, George. The Senecan Amble: A Study in Prose Form from
Bacon to Collier. Chicago: University of Chicago Press, 1951.

                                 Milton

Barker, Arthur E. Milton and the Puritan Dilemma, 1641–1660. Toronto:
University of Toronto Press, 1941.
Darbishire, Helen, ed. Early Lives of Milton. London: Constable, 1932.
Fink, Zera S. "The Development of Milton's Political Thought." PMLA
57 (1942): 705–36.
Frye, Northrop. The Return of Eden. Toronto: University of Toronto
Press, 1965.
Grossman, Allen. "Milton's Sonnet 'On the Late Massacre in Piemont':
A Note on the Vulnerability of Persons in a Revolutionary Situation."
In Literature in Revolution, ed. Charles Newman and George Abbot
White. A special issue of Triquarterly 23–24 (1972): 283–301.
Hamilton, K. G. "The Structure of Milton's Prose." In Language and
Style in Milton: A Symposium in Honor of the Tercentenary of "Para-
dise Lost," ed. Ronald D. Emma and John T. Shawcross. New York:
Frederick Ungar, 1967, pp. 304–32.
Lewalski, Barbara K. "Milton: Political Beliefs and Polemical Methods,
1659–60." PMLA 74 (1959): 191–202.
Masson, David. The Life of John Milton, 7 vols. London: Macmillan &
Co., 1859–94.
Parker, William R. Milton: A Biography, 2 vols. Oxford: Oxford Uni-
versity Press, 1968.
——. Milton's Contemporary Reputation. Columbus: Ohio State Uni-
versity Press, 1940.
Sirluck, Ernest. "Milton's Political Thought: The First Cycle." MP 61
(1964): 209–24.
Weaver, Richard. "Milton's Heroic Prose." In The Ethics of Rhetoric.
Chicago: Henry Regnery Co., 1953, pp. 143–63.
Wolfe, Don M. Milton in the Puritan Revolution. New York: Thomas
Nelson and Sons, 1941.

INDEX

For individual tracts discussed at length, see the Table of Contents. Tracts discussed briefly or mentioned in passing are listed here as separate entries.

Eikonoklastes, 86–89 passim; and
Restoration, 94, 98, 99; in Readie
and Easie Way, 104; and Areopagitica, 126
Loose syntax: and Milton, 3, 4, 122;
and Browne, 4; Milton and Browne
contrasted, 4–9; participials, 5–7,
16, 22; appositions, 7–8; trailing
clauses, 8, 18–19; ascends to oh
altitudo, 8–9, 43; and private
energies, 9; interpolated clauses,
16, 22, 23; and Lilburne, 16–17.
See also Syntax
Low style. See Plain style
Luther, Martin, 83

Mailer, Norman, 116
Marx, Karl, 116
Milton, Mary Powell, 54
Milton's poems: and political ac-
tion, 1, 2, 113–14, 119; Paradise
Lost, 2, 111, 113–14, 119, 127;
Comus, 18; Paradise Regained,
34, 98, 113; Sonnet XI, 65; Sonnet
XII, 65; Samson Agonistes, 113
Mixed state: and Milton, 99
Modest Confuter, 18, 48–53 passim
Monarchy: Milton opposes, 100–
101, 105–106, 107–108
Monck, General George, 98, 99, 113
Montaigne, Michel de, 16
Mosaic Law, 35; and divorce, 56,
57, 62–64 passim

New Model Army, 21, 24–26 passim,
74, 94

Of Prelatical Episcopacy, 34
Of True Religion, 129
Orwell, George, 1–2, 115, 116

Pagan prose: authoritarian implications, 117–18
Palmer, Herbert (Presbyterian
divine), 66
Pathetic proof, 54, 57, 61, 84. See
also Emotion; Reason

Paul, Saint, 44, 59, 62, 65, 72, 126
Persona: in Apology, 48, 51–53; in
divorce tracts, 55; in Areopagitica,
66–69; in Eikonoklastes, 86, 90; in
Treatise and Means, 98; in Readie
and Easie Way, 101, 105, 107, 109,
110–11
Plain style: egalitarian implications, 115–19. See also Leveller
prose
Plato, 35, 36
Pragmatism: in Readie and Easie
Way, 99–100
Prelacy: Milton attacks, 7–8, 27–
34 passim, 45–46, 47, 50, 51;
bishops excluded from House of
Lords, 49; Archbishop Laud
impeached, 49
Presbyterians, 17, 44; Milton at-
tacks, 22–23, 54, 66, 67–69, 73,
74, 76–84 passim, 90; and the
English Revolution, 24, 26; Milton
supports, 27, 35, 46, 53; supported
Restoration, 98, 103; and Readie
and Easie Way, 99
Pride's Purge, 98
Prophetic wrath: in Reformation,
28–34
Prose style: and political meaning,
1–2, 115
Protestantism: defined in Trea-
tise, 95
Protestant Reformation, 28, 67
Prynne, William (Puritan spokes-
man), 17, 69
Puritan coalition, 20, 74
Puritan Revolution. See English
Revolution
Puritans. See Independents; Pres-
byterians

Rainborough, Thomas (Leveller
agitator), 24, 25
Reason: and imagination in Areopagitica, 29–30, 45, 69–71; and
imagination in Reason, 35–45;
and emotion in divorce tracts,